WORLD POLITICS
THEORIES & APPROACHES

WORLD POLITICS

Theories & Approaches

By

Puran Chandra

AKANSHA PUBLISHING HOUSE
NEW DELHI-110 059 (INDIA)

AKANSHA PUBLISHING HOUSE
R-37B, Vani Vihar, Uttam Nagar
New Delhi-110059
Phones: 25640621, 9811582579
Email: ektabooks@yahoo.com

World Politics: Theories & Approaches

First Published 2004

ISBN 81-87606-45-2

PRINTED IN INDIA

Published by M.P. Misra for Akansha Publishing House, New Delhi-110059 and Printed at Tarun Offset Press, Delhi.

Contents

Preface

The World politics has had a chequered history. It is the Europe which has mainly determined the course of world politics or international politics. War being a daily business of men, many wars have been fought in the past. The First World War was the greatest in its magnitude, dimension and destruction. The causes of war can be categorically summarised as—formation of alliance, treatment of Bismarck, economic rivalry, colonial expansion, rise of militant nationalism, and lack of any world organisation. The ghastly drama of the unprecedented World War came to an end in 1918. Out of nearly 65 million participants, 13 million died in action leaving 22 million people wounded and approximately 270,000,000,000 dollars were wasted.

With the Treaty of Versailles in 1919 with Germany, several treaties were also concluded. Emergence and eclipse of League of Nations, Second World War, foundation of United Nations Organisation (UNO), freedom of various European colonies in the East, Bipolarity in world politics, sense of nationalism, economic development and international trade, were other major events which shaped and reshaped the international politics. After dismantling of the USSR, and acquisition of nuclear weapons by many nations and emergence of WTO in the last decades of 20th century, the world politics again took new turn. With the dawn of new century toward unipolarity, new faces of imperialism, extreme faces of terrorism and religious fundamentalism etc. are heading towards reshaping the world politics once again.

Here, in this book we have presented an historical account of theories and approaches to the world politics, which obviously will interest the scholars in the area of international relations and politics. We have given a compact account of events, already told/retold by various scholars of repute.

We hope, this endeavour will prove of interest and use to students, researchers, teachers and the aspirants appearing for various competitive examinations conducted by the UPSC and state public service commissions. Finally, a word of acknowledgement. I owe a deep sense of gratitude to all the great scholars on whose creations, the present work is woven. The publishers also deserve appreciation for undertaking the publication.

—PC

1

Introduction to Political System

The concept of 'political system' is frequently used in the field of political analysis. Although this term replaces the terms used in older texts such as 'state'. 'nation' or 'government', it involves something more than mere style of nomenclature. It reflects a new way of pondering at political phenomena.

The modern political analysis, through the concept of political system, gives a comprehensive framework of analysis for dealing effectively with political phenomena in all kinds of societies, irrespective of its culture, degree of modernization and size. As such the concept of 'political system' has required wide currency because it directs its attention to the entire scope of political activities within a society, regardless of where in the society such activities may be located. When we come across the concept very often, a question automatically comes to the mind as to what actually is a political system? How do we define its boundary? What gives the political system its special identity? Before going into the elaboration of the complexities of political system, it would be necessary to have an insight into what is meant by a system and how a political system developed in political analysis?

The idea of a system originated in the writings of L.V. Bertallanfy who first used the term in Biology to describe different parts of human body on the basis of their functions viz. the circulatory system, the digestive system etc. A system is basically a set of units standing in interaction with each other, having close relationship among themselves. Collin Cherry puts it as 'a whole compounded of many parts – an ensemble of attitudes'. System is thus a kind of collective entity with interdependence between parts, components and processes that involve regularities of relationship. It has been created to discharge certain specific functions. It has got a boundary beyond which it is non-existent. The different units of a system are separate and distinguishable in nature; but at the same time they are inter-related and inter-dependent and as such interact with each other.

Development of Political System

The principle of 'General systems theory', originally developed in natural sciences, was applied to the study of political phenomena with some transformations made first by anthropologists followed by the sociologists. Such transformation in the general systems theory was inevitable because the social scientist wanted to move ahead with the help of this theory. The principles and terms of general systems theory was first modified by the writings of famous anthropologists like W.R. Ashby, Norbest Weiner, Emile Durkheim, A.R. Radcliff Brown, Malinowski etc. They all significantly contributed to the theoretical growth of systems approach. It was further modified by the sociologists like Robert K. Merton, George C. Homans, Talcott Parsons etc. As a result of such alterations and modifications, the general systems theory has developed a set of basic principles which is applicable to a wide range of empirical investigations. Parsons developed the technical idea of a social system. Drawing upon the inspirations from the anthropologists and sociologists in general, and Talcott Parsons in particular, David Easton applied the study of system in the analysis of political phenomena and in his approach of study he used for the first time the new concept called the 'political system'. He not only developed the concept of political system in political analysis, but also built up the 'input-output' model which still remains as an important legendary milestone in modern political analysis. Following Talcott Parsons and David Easton, Gabriel Almond also discussed at length about political system and gave a comprehensive characteristic of it on the basis of a structural - functional analysis. While Easton and Almond concentrated on the application of political system to national politics, Mortan Kaplan moved further and applied the concept in international field of politics.

Definitions of Political System

According to Max Weber, "a political system is human community that successfully claims the monopoly of legitimate use of physical coercion within a given territory."

Lasswell and Kaplan say "Shaping and sharing of power is the main concern of political system with the help of threat for actual use of severe deprivation for non-compliance."

David Easton say, " a political system is the set of interactions abstracted from the totality of social behaviour through which authoritative of value are made and implemented for society."

Robert Dahl defines political system as "any persistent pattern of human relationship that involves to a significant extent power, rule and authority."

Gabriel A. Almond opines, " Political system is that system of interaction to be found in all independent societies which performs the function of integration and adaptation by means of employment or threat of employment of more or less legitimate physical compulsion."

To conclude, all these definitions imply legitimate heavy sanctions; the rightful power to punish, to enforce, to compel. Hence legitimate force is the thread that runs through the actions of political system, giving it its special quality and importance, and its coherence as a system. Political system includes governmental institutions and also all interactions which affect the use of legitimate physical coercion.

Eastonian View of Political System

David Easton was the first political scientist who developed the concept of 'political system' as a systematic framework of analysis of political phenomena. Political scientists, before him studied political phenomena in isolation that never led to useful study because totally neglecting the environment around. Easton found political system as the most suitable unit through which all political processes and forces could be analysed. He viewed political system as a guided missile which automatically hits the target and as such employed the systems theory to make a macro-analysis of political system. By making political system a basic unit of analysis,

Easton wanted to build up a unified political theory capable of explaining the behaviour of both national an international systems. Not only he was interested in this but also he was equally concerned with the study of survival or persistence of the system itself against the inevitable stress that they face. At the same time, he was more interested in analyzing how the system persists in both stable and unstable environment.

With all these motives in mind, Easton started analyzing political system at length from his 'input-output' model that exhibits the following salient features of a political system:

1. A political system is always adaptive in nature i.e. it is constantly receiving from other systems as well as from its environment, a stream of events, which influence the system as a whole. It is with the help of these information that the political system try to cope up with the environmental hazards and regulate its own behaviour. As such it has well-responding and self regulating mechanism by which it can change, correct and readjust its processes and structures to maintain equilibrium.
2. A political system is just one among various social systems it functions within a boundary beyond which it is non-existent. It is the very presence of the boundary which separates a political system from all other systems.
3. Political system, apart from being a system in itself, consists of subsystems such as mediating groups that are involved in the decision making process. These groups may not have the character of political organization and hence can be termed as 'para-political systems.'
4. A political system always remain subject to challenges from forces operating in the environment with which it is required to cope with. These challenges are the stress which expresses itself either in the form of a demand or support. Demand stress resulted either from the failure of the system to cope up with its environment or from the incapability of the system to deal with a particular range of demands made upon it. Support stress, on the other hand, may result form the split or dissention in the

political elite and its overall impact is the loss of support given to the system by its members.

5. A political system is closely linked with a feedback process. It is a mechanism which transmits the consequent reaction of the environment of the authoritative decisions (outputs), either positive or negative character, into the system (as inputs) that will further determine the subsequent outputs. It is on account of this feed back mechanism that a political system persists and maintain equilibrium.
6. A political system, in order to maintain equilibrium, always underwent an input-conversion-output process which gives life and meaning to the political system. Inputs are the demands made upon the system as well as the support given to it (political system). The conversion process gives the political system the capacity to cope with the demands made upon it by successfully transforming the demands into policy outlines. By output it means the authoritative decisions made by the men at power.
7. A political system receives support from political communities, regimes or constitutional order and authorities. Political community means the group of people living together with willingness to cooperate in solving their issues. The constitutional order implies those set of impersonal rules which determines the norms and structures of the political organization. Authority means the people who are entrusted with the power to allocate values for the society.
8. No political system can survive without structural bases viz. political Parties, electoral machinery and such non-institutional arrangements as attitudes of the people their political beliefs.

However, in spite of the fact that the Eastonian concept of political system still remains as a search light for political sociologists in so far as it provides a comprehensive framework for analysis of political phenomena against a wider societal background, it is not out of criticism. Eugene Mecham criticized him. "Like parsons, Easton does not think of a theory in terms of explanation, but in terms of the creation of a conceptual frame work. Hence it is a highly abstract structure that is logically suspect, conceptually fuzzy and empirically, almost useless". Easton has also been criticized for his empty vision of politics because he has shown a very little interest in the individuals. To Paul F. Kress, " in Easton's analysis, there is lack of substance, artificial nature of the system and disappearance of boundaries."

The Input-Output Model of Easton

The whole concept of political system, for David Easton, revolves round his input-output model of political analysis. He has four assumptions on political system such as:

(1) A system is distinguishable from its environment in which it exists and it is open to the influences from the environment;

(2) It is useful to view political system as a system of behaviour.

(3) There is a feedback mechanism in the political system by which the system has the capacity to regulate itself.

(4) The system is responsive in character i.e. there is a variation in structures and processes in the system to cope up with the environment. Thus the political system is constructive and not destructive in nature.

Relying on these assumptions Easton selected political system as the basis unit of analysis through which all political processes could be studies. The political system operates through the input-output model. Hence a proper understanding of the operational aspect of the political system will be incomplete unless and until the input-output model is taken into consideration. From an indepth review, the model includes the following elements in its ambit which need a thorough but brief description:

(a) The environment; (b) The Self-regulating mechanism; (c) The inputs; d) The conversion process; (e) The outputs; and (f) The feedback process.

1. The Environment

Environment is the first element of Easton's model. A political system does not exist in vacuum, rather it is surrounded by a vast array of environment which influences the performance of the political system. It consists of both social as well as physical surroundings. To Easton, the environment may be intra-societal or extra-societal.

a) The Intra-social Environment: The Intra-social environment consists of a set of behaviours, attitudes and ideas. It is of four types such as – the ecological, biological, personality and social environment. Ecological environment refers to the physical surrounding and the non-organic conditions of human existence. It also includes the geographical elements and their nature. Biological environment includes the genetics and hereditary traits of the individual, the elements of cooperation and coexistence that are inherited from the parents. Personality of an individual also constitutes the intra-societal environment insofar as the personality of individual leaders can have a deep and unbelievable impact on the political system itself. Social environment includes the cultural and economic system which exist within the society.

b) The Extra-societal Environment: The extra-societal environment constitutes the international political system, international ecological system and international social system. All those international systems exert a deep influence upon the performance of the political system as a whole for the political system is open and adaptive in nature, subjected to exposure to the influences in the environment.

A political system is always subjected to challenges from its environment and it tries to overcome the challenges by making necessary value adjustments. The political system also receives the energy to activate itself from the environment. Every political system continue to persist and maintain its equilibrium even in the face of stress and strains coming from the environment, thereby giving itself the quality of dynamism.

2) The Self-Regulating Mechanism

The self regulating mechanism regulates the behaviour and activities of the political system even in the face of challenges thrown to it from the environment. To Easton, every political system undergoes changes and the degree of change determines the failure, success and continuity of the system. So long as the authoritative allocation of values are successful the system persists. A changed political system also persists because every political system is self-regulatory in nature. There are four self regulating mechanisms, cultural mechanism, reduction mechanism and communication mechanism.

a) Gate Keeping Mechanism: It is designed to regulate the flow of inputs from entering into the political system and therefore, operates at the boundary of the political system it shunts out the weeded one from the boundary of the political system on the pretext that they are either not proper demands to be made on political system or if accepted, it would jeopardise the very existence of the political system itself. It allows only those inputs to enter into the political system which it thinks proper to be communicated and therefore get itself converted into articulated demands.

b) Communication Mechanism: This is a mechanism which made its very presence within the political system itself and helps in diluting the articulated demands called interests (that comes into the political system) in a process of decision making and communicate the values allocated (decisions made) to the environment (society) and again communicate the reactions of the people on the decisions to the political system through the feedback loop.

c) Cultural Mechanism: Such a mechanism checks the flow of anti-cultural demands from entering into the political system and therefore, also operates at the boundary level.

d) Inputs: As Easton's whole concept of political system revolves round the input-output, the study of 'Inputs' generate much interest. Inputs are the pressures of all kind coming from the environment which keeps the political system in motion and there by help it to overcome the stress and strains coming form the environment, both intra-societal and extra-societal.

e) Reduction Mechanism: It is a mechanism which operates at the inner boundary of the political system. It converts the articulated demands that flow into the political system into specific issues called interests.

In general, while demand are the goals of the political system, support provides the resources to carry out the goals. No demand can be responded well unless support is received from the society.

(4) Conversion Process

The manner and mechanism through which a political system converts the inputs (i.e. the articulated demands or interests) into outputs (i.e. the value allocations or decisions) and thereby respond to the challenges in the environment is called the conversion process. The articulated interests are converted into authoritative value allocations (or decisions) after a through process of selection, rearrangement and voting.

The effectiveness of the conversion process depends upon the nature of the political system itself. If the political system is primarily regulative and extractive in character, then the demands coming from the environment is suppressed and remains mostly, unresponded. On the otherhand, if the political system is distributive and responsive, the demands are equally responded and values are allocated authoritatively forth with.

(5) Outputs

The outputs of a political system are "the authoritative decisions and actions of the leaders in power that influence the allocation of values for the society." It is the result of the conversion process acting upon a variety of demands and expressing itself in the form of rules, regulations, actions, laws and so on.

(6) Feed-back Process

Easton says, "the outputs not only help in influencing the events in the society, but also helps to determine each succeeding round of inputs that find its way into the political system through the process of feedback loop." The feedback process, thus, as the name suggests entails that the information regarding each round of outputs are fedback to the political system through inputs that express in the form of demands and support. Through this process of feedback loop, the political system takes the advantage of knowing the new developments in the society as a reaction to its output and thereby try to adjust its future course of action so that the political system could best adapted to changing conditions, maintain its equilibrium and persist in the face of stress and strains coming from the environment. Feedback has two aspects – negative and goal changing. While negative aspect deals with the regulation of an error, the goal changing aspect concerned with the problem of purposive redirection.

Input-output model of Easton is also known as the **black box model** because it is not known how the inputs are converted into outputs.

THE ALMONDIAN VIEW OF POLITICAL SYSTEM

Gabriel A. Almond was the modern political scientist after Easton, who worked with the concept of political system and tried to give it a more precise, clear cut and value oriented definition. His approach of political system is more empirical his predecessors insofar as he exposed the weaknesses of other definitions on political system and gave his own which is more comprehensive and analytical and thereby suits the study of political phenomena in all kinds of societies, irrespective of structures, functions and cultures. His political system includes not only the state or governmental institutions but all structures in their political aspects – viz. family, clan, religious groups etc.

For giving an empirical touch to his version on political system, almond took up the definitions of other writers and refuted them one after another by exposing its weakness. First of all, he took up the definition of Max Weber that political system is a human community that successful claims the monopoly of legitimate use of physical force within a given territory. No doubt Almond agrees with Weber that legitimate force is a thread that runs through political system, giving it a special meaning, yet he accepts this definition as partial insofar as this definition is more applicable to states than to political systems. He then, took up the definition of Lasswell and Kaplan that political system is concerned with the shaping and sharing of power with the help of threat for actual use of "severe deprivation for non-compliance". But Almond rejects this view on the ground that they have failed to explain what by 'Severe deprivation' they actually mean. Thereafter, he took up the definition of Easton that it is a set of interactions through which authoritative allocation of values are made and implemented for society. Though Almond accepted this view as comprehensive yet he feels that Easton has made authoritativeness as the sole characteristic of a political system. He is of the view that political system not only performs the function of authoritative decision as observed by Easton, but also certain other functions which provides legitimacy to the acts of the authority in power. Therefore Almond defines political system as "that system of interaction to be found in all independent societies which performs the function of integration and adaptation by means of employment or threat of employment of more or less legitimate physical compulsion." While giving such a definition of political system, Almond has three things in this mind:

a) Political system is a concrete whole which influence and in turn, being influenced by the environment;

b) In a political system, the interaction took place nor between the individuals but between their roles; and

c) Political system, as an open system, performs different types of functions of integration and adaptation.

Salient Features of a Political System

According to Almond a political system has got three properties – comprehensiveness, interdependence and existence of boundaries.

(a) ***Comprehensiveness***: It means political system includes all interactions (both inputs and outputs) which affect the use of threat of use of physical coercion. It not only deals with the structures based on constitutional and legal foundations but also equally stresses on the informal organizations and anoemic phenomena which have their impact on the political system.

(b) ***Interdependence***: it means, political system, being a whole, consists of a set of sub systems which are inter related and inter-dependent on each other i.e. a change in the magnitude and quality of one variable has its direct impact on other subsystems as well as on the political system as a whole and thus, affects their performance process.

(c) ***Existence of Boundaries***: A political system starts somewhere and ends somewhere. A boundary is a point where a political system is distinguished from other systems. It is the inexact live drawn between the social system and political system through which diffused demands are translated into articulated interests – thereby giving support to the functioning of the political system.

Almond says that all political systems, whether primitive or modern, developed or developing, have political structures which performs different types of political functions. The interaction between these political structures and political functions help in maintaining both internal and external order.

To Almond, every political system has the following four features:

1) ***Universality of political structures*:** That is, the same political structures perform the same political functions in different political systems, through with varying degree or frequency.

2) ***Mixed culture*:** All political systems combine both primitive and modern elements and thus represents a mixed system in cultural sense. Every political system represents a curious blend of mixture of both traditionality and rationality and thus always finds itself in a state of flux and change (i.e. transitional stage) in which cultural changes took place.

3) ***Universality of political structures*:** That is, the same type of functions are performed in all political systems. As such, the overall performance of the political system depends upon the roles played by the structures in their political context.

4) ***Multi-functionality of political structures*:** That is, all political structures, irrespective of the degree of specialization, performs more than one function because, it is difficult to confine any political structure with one and only one function in modern period. For Example, courts not only adjudicate but also legislate; bureaucracy acts as a source of legislation; legislature affects both administration and adjudication political parties and pressure groups initiate legislation and participate in national administration etc.

Thus political system always remains prone to be influenced by environmental factors; and by making necessary value adjustments, a political system always try to cope up with the stress and strains coming from the environment thus maintains equilibrium. Almond also gave his own **input-output model** of political system that strategically differs from that of Easton in so far as while Easton talked about only two types of input functions (i.e. demands and support) and the governmental decisions as output functions, Almond prescribes a comprehensive list of four input functions (i.e. political socialization and recruitment, interest articulation, interest aggregation, and political communication) and three output functions (i.e. rule making, rule application and rule adjudication). Thus, we have given here a theoretical analysis of political system to understand better the International Politics.

2

Fundamental Political Concepts

Authority, Power, Legitimacy, and Leadership are the major basic political concepts, which are being given an elaborate treatment here.

POWER

Power is an inherent and indispensable part of human activity. Max Weber defined power as " the chances of a man or a group of men to realize their own will in a communal action even against the resistance of others who are participating in the action." Power is therefore, an aspect of social relationship. An individual or group do not hold power is therefore, power over other.

Dowse and Hughes says that "politics is about power. Politics occurs when there are differentials aspect, any social relationship that involves power differential is political."

Sociologists often distinguish between two forms of power—authority and coercion. Authority is that form of power which is accepted a legitimate, right and just, and therefore, is obeyed on that basis. On the other hand, coercion is that form of power which is not regarded as legitimate by those subject to it. However, it has often been argued that both the forms of power are ultimately based on physical force, whether their power is regarded as legitimate or not.

Eric Kauffman says that " the essence of state is the development, increase and display of power". So political power is one which operates within the periphery of the state and its institutions. It is recognized that the state can afford to wield the strongest power since it is able to reserve for itself the right to apply the severest sanctions like imprisonment and capital punishment. Besides this, in all other respects, there is basically no difference between the power of the state and the power to be found at any other level of society. Political power, in fact, is conditioned by the social process. This implies that political power will differ according to the variations in the nature and working of the social processes.

In his book *Political Power*, Charles Merriam evolved his concept of 'power' in place of Arthur F. Bentely's concept of ' interests'. However, he did not draw a sharp line of distinction between authority and power.

Bertrand Russell in his books "*Political Power – A New Social Analysis*" (1937) and "Authority and Individuals" (1939), described the role of power in strongest terms. He defined power as "a capacity to produce intended effects." Russel is of the opinion that equality of power, secured by the dispersion of power, was a more important condition of human freedom than the equality of wealth. In communism, he saw the establishment of a bureaucratic aristocracy concentrating authority in its own hand and creating a regime just as oppressive and cruel as that of capitalism.

George Catlin is of the opinion that power is central to political science. Catlin adopts the Weberian concept of politics as the struggle for power or of influencing of those, in power.

Harold Lasswell and Abraham Kaplan's book "*Power and Society: A Framework for Political Enquiry*" provides the most detailed analysis of the concept of power. They wrote that the concept of power is perhaps, the most fundamental in the whole of political science and the political process is nothing but shaping sharing, distribution and exercise of political power. Power is inextricably related to influence. In Lasswell's analysis, power is a value in its own right and is also an instrument in the realization of other values. Anything and everything that man wants, is described by Lasswell as 'Values'. To him, power is both an end in itself and also a means to achieve an end. To the question, what do men want, Lasswell answers in terms of his distributive analysis – " most of what there is to get." He speaks of a trilogy of values income, safety and deference, which is comparable to the Hobbes' approach as competence, diffidence and glory.

Thus, Power is not only an end in itself, but also is a means or instrument for the achievement of other values. Values are interdependent in the sense that if one is able to acquire certain values in substantial measure, he is in a position to acquire other values. Power is rarely derived for its own sake rather it is thought of, as an instrumental value or as a necessary pre-requisite for realizing other values in the society. In political aspect, Lasswell defines power as participation in decision making process which is an interpersonal activity. Thus Lasswell's power is distributive and the aim of political science is to determine how and on what basis the power is distributed.

R. H. Tawney defined power as the capacity of an individual or group of individuals to modify the conduct of other individuals or groups in a manner in which the former desires."

Power and Influence

Influence is a person's capacity to affect other's behaviour in a way willed by the former. Hence the exercise of influence consists in affecting the policies of others than the self.

One can broadly distinguish between influence and power. While influence is a broad concept, power is specific case. Power is a specific case. Power is a special kind of influence. It is the actual use or a threat of use of sanctions that differentiates power from influence in general. However, in influence, both persuasion and compulsions are there.

To measure influence, one has to take note of its weight, domain and scope. The weight of influence is the degree to which policies are affected; the domain of influence deals with the persons whose policies are affected; where as, the scope of influence includes the values implicated in the policies. There are instances of influences, where the probability of compliance on part of the influenced, is very high. This requires a little effort on part of the actor influencing to establish his influence. This kind of influence is called spontaneous influence. Again, there may be situations, where the probability of compliance, being extremely low. Requires a considerable effort on part of the actor influencing to establish his influence. This effort, invariably involves, an actual use or a threat of use of sanctions. Such kind of influence is called coercive influence and power, is the other name of coercive influence.

Power is thus, a special kind of influence. It is the capacity to affect other's behaviour by the actual use or threat of use of sanctions. The sanctions involved in power, need not always have to be an actual or threatened deprivation inflicting penalties and losses on others. They may also be applied in the form of giving or promising to give rewards like wealth or honour etc. the former is an instance of negative sanction, whereas, the latter, is a case of the use of positive sanctions. The positive sanctions, in the form of a promise of reward, however, may in some cases, got transformed into negative sanctions.

Ingredients of Power

Since power is the capacity to affect other's behaviour, it is basically relational, and not a simple personal property. One can have power only over others.

Power is relational implies that it is also behavioural. Because it wants to change the behaviour of others. If power consists in an inter-relation between two actors, then certainly, that interrelationship can only be understood in terms of one actor's manifest behaviour as affecting the manifest behaviour of others. It is also behavioural because it is liable to measurement and comparative assessment. Power, in addition to being relational and behavioural, is also situational. That is to say, to know power, one has necessarily to relate it to a specific situation or to a specific role. An actor's power in one particular situation or role may vary from that of in others.

Finally, power is also reciprocal. In implies that the relationship of power is invariably of a raciprocal nature. As such, if a controls B, then B, to some extent at least, also controls A. so while A exerts influence over B, B, is also, to some extent, more or less, exerts influence on A and tries to implement its own will.

Fundamentals of Power

Power have different bases which differ from culture to culture and also from one political structure to another. Within a culture, certain factors such as wealth, control over the instruments of violence, skill, faith, loyalty, habit, apathy, interest and power over one issue area may often serve as a good base for extending power to other issue areas. The power base, coupled with the ability to use this power constitutes the capability for power. In addition, there must be a will or desire on part of the actor influencing to control the actions of others. Power emerges whenever, the capability of power is combined with will to affect the behaviour of others.

Everybody in every society has a tendency to extend his power. The extent to which power seeking will be met with success depends on how much capability and will the power seeker possesses. Once power is acquired, the power holder tries power, once secured, can be used to achieve a variety of ends like fame, reverence, security, respect, affection, wealth and many other values. So he, who has acquired power, will invariably try to extend it. This search fro further power by one power holder may be checked by similar search by other power holder. The powerful is subdued by the more powerful. Hence power limits power. Power, however, is also limited by other factors.

In *Modern Political Analysis*, Robert A. Dahl discusses four different ways of detecting power relations in a particular situation. In the first place, one may try to measure power by necessarily relating it to an office assuming that power operates only within a framework of formal office. But focus on formal office may often be inadequate to grasp the nature and extent of power since in many cases power does not remain in formal office, but is, instead, wielded by forces laying beyond them and managing to control the office holder from a distance. The second technique of detecting power is to concentrate on actual decision making process. This technique enquires into the nature and level of people's participation in the actual decision making process. The fourth technique is to weigh the activities of different participants in the decision making and coming to a judgement about the nature and extent of power after carefully comparing these activities.

While observing a power relation, one has to keep in mind three aspects of power – weight, scope and domain of political power. The weight of power means the degree of participation in the making of decisions while its scope means the values at stake and the domain of power refers to the persons over whom power is exercised.

According to Robert Dahl, " A has power over B to the extent that he can get B to do something that B would not otherwise do". Here the main focus, is not on the actions and intensions of the power holder, i.e. the actor exercising power, but on the enquiry as to whether the power addressee i.e. the actor against whom the power is exercised, does something in opposition to his own intension. Unless there is this opposition, there cannot be a power relation. Dahl puts his thrust in this way because he considers sanctions as the most important attributes of power.

However, difficulty arises if the power addressee does not agree to the directions of the power holder. Herbert Goldhamer and Edward Shills, in their analysis of power in their book "Types of power and Status" have dealt with this problem kneatly. To them, a person may be said to have power to the extent that he influences the behaviour of others in accordance with his own intensions." The difference between this definition and that of Dahl is evident. While Dahl's emphasis was on the power addressee, the emphasis of Goldhamer and Shills' is on the power holder, on his own intensions. On the basis of the criterion provided by Goldhamer and Shills', one has first, to determine the intensions of the power holder, and then see, whether the policies adopted by the power addressee follow these intensions. If they do, then the former will be regarded as having power over latter. Thus the definition of Goldhamer and Shill's seems more attractive and influential than that of the Dahl's.

Prof. A.K. Mukhopadhyaya have delineated another problem which arise when the power holder does not communicate to the power addressee about his intensions. The answer goes negatively because the intensions of power holder have to be effective in order to constitute power relation. So it is not possible if these intensions are not communicated to the power addressee. Thus there must be some communication or contact between the power holder and the power addressee. In order to make an actor powerful, his intensions along with an act on his part to communicate these intensions are very much essential.

Functionalist Approach to Power

Max Weber defines power as "the chances of a man or a

number of men to realize their own will in a communal action even against the resistance of others who are participating in the action". Weber's definition of power implies that those who hold power, do so at the expenses of others. It suggests that there is a fixed amount of power and therefore, if some hold power, others do not. This view is known as the 'Constant sum' concept of power. Weber's definition also implies that power holder will tend to use power to further their own interests. Sociologists argue that power is used to further the sectional interests of the power holder which are in conflict with the interests of those subject to that power. To them, therefore, power is used mainly for the exploitation and oppression of some by others.

Talcott Parsons rejects the 'constant sum' concept of power and the view that power is employed into the furtherance of sectional interests. Rather than seeing power as something which some hold at the expense of others, Parsons regards it as something possessed by the society as whole. As such, power is a 'generalized facility or resources in the society'. In particular, it is the capacity to mobilize the resources of the society for the attainment of goals for which a general 'public' commitment has been made. In this sense, the amount of power in society is measured by the degree to which collective goals are realized. Thus, the greater the efficiency of a social system for achieving the goals defined by its members, the more power exists in the society.

Marxian Approach to Power

Marxian analysis of power provides a radical alternative to Parsons' functionalist approach. It rejects the view that power is a societal resource held in trust and directed by those in authority for the benefit for all. Instead, power is seen, to be held by a particular group in the society at the expense of the rest of the society. This is a 'Zero-sum' concept of power because a net gain in the power of the dominant group represents a net loss in the power of the rest of the society. The dominant group uses this power to further its own interest. These interests are indirect conflict with the interests of those subject to its power. This is radically different from the picture presented by Parsons in which rules and ruled are pulled together for the benefit of the society as a whole, undivided by any fundamental conflict of interests.

The sources of power in society lies in the economic infrastructure. In all stratified society the forces of production are owned and controlled by a minority, the ruling class. The relationship to the forces of production provides the basis of its dominance. It therefore, follows that the only way to return power to people involves communal ownership of the forces of production. Since everyone will now share the same relationship to the forces of production, power will be shared by all members of society.

Marxists term the use of power to exploit others as *coercion*. It is seen as illegitimate use of power because it forces the subject class to submit to a situation which is against their interest.

AUTHORITY

Power is the predisposition which makes the application of force or sanctions for the resolution of social conflicts. Although power involves the use of severest sanctions by actual employment or threat of employment of physical coercion, yet it is not the cause for stability of political power. Political power is stable and permanent not only because it is based on sanction, but because it is based on one's compliance, on a belief on part of the person obeying that it is proper to obey the commands. Political power is strengthened by legitimacy. When political power is clothed in legitimacy it is called authority in the political sphere. Authority, is therefore, a special kind of power; power, when legitimized gives rise to authority. Authority is the institutionalized right to issue commands and employ power.

Due to its presence in the political, social and economic sphere, authority has different dimensions – social, economic and political. In the economic dimension authority deals with superiority in matters of production, distribution and exchange. In social sphere, it means the top position in social hierarchy. In the field of management and public administration, authority has been regarded as the right to issue commands.

Meaning of Authority

According to Herbert Simon, authority comes into existence when the subordinates give up their own freedom to choose one of the various alternatives available to them. To him, the authority relation exists only when there occurs an actual change in the behaviour of the subordinates. The superior takes the decision and communicate those to the subordinates with the expectation that they will be accepted by the subordinates so authority relation involves a two way relationship an expectation of obedience and an willingness to obey.

According to Bertrand De Jouvenel, "authority is a faculty of inducting assents. To follow an authority is a voluntary assent ends."

F. Hannah Arendf writes, "authority means power based on consent. Its hallmark is unquestioning recognition by those who are asked to obey; neither coercion nor persuation is needed."

Michell regards authority as " a capacity innate or acquired, for exercising ascendancy over a group." It is a manifestation of power and implies obedience on part of those subject to it.

MacIver says, "authority is often being defined as power, the power to command obedience."

Frederich defines authority as "a quality of communication that possesses the potentiality of reasoned elaboration." A possesses authority because B regards A's communication as authoritative. It means B recognized A's command as reasonable in terms of his own values.

Aspects of Authority

Authority, in political sphere, is invariably related with political system. In other words, when power is exercised by the political system, it creates authority. So in political systems, power is always associated with the authority. But in all other social systems, very often power is found to be detached from authority. So in social sphere, there may be authority without power or power without authority. For Example, a local hooligan may have power for harassing his neighbors, but no authority for that. So there may be a clear distinction between power and authority in social sphere. But in political level, both of them are integratedly related with each other related with each other making one impossible without other.

Barring political level, in all other levels authority and power differ from each other. While authority means the ability to get consent, power refers to the capacity to influence the behaviour of others. People obey authority because they feel the rightness of the position of the person who exercises power.

Nature of Authority

The formal theory of authority maintains that authority is the right to issue commands. Authority flows from the superior to the subordinate, making up the organizational hierarchy. On the other hand, acceptance theory relates to the behavioural school of human relations and according to it, the successful authority depends on the acceptance of order by the subordinates. Here the subordinate tends to make room in their mind for receiving the orders of communication from their superiors and comply with them without reasoning and opposition.

The most important element of authority is the concept of legitimaçy which means the ability to evoke or create compliance without the use of coercion or force or any form of sanctions. This is necessary to establish a durable power relationship between the superior and the subordinates. Because the power addressee or the subordinate cannot always go on submitting himself to the dictates of power holder for fear of sanctions so what is necessary then, is to create an atmosphere where the power addressee himself voluntarily agree to be abide by the orders of the power holder because he feels that the power holder has a right to issue orders.

Prof. Mukhopadhayaya opines, "authority may be defined as the recognized right to exercise power irrespective of the sanctions the power holder is able to apply.' That is to say, an actor has right to power not when there is no bar in his trying to affect the behaviour of others, but when the latter voluntarily agree to have their position affected by the former, there by giving him a right to compliance.

It is not only essential for establishing a durable power relationship, but also necessary because it is very much convenient and useful for a power holder as it involves the application of minimum resources. To exercise power, by means of sanctions, is quite expensive. Authority, not being necessarily dependent on the use of sanctions, avoids such large expenditure of resources. Robert

Dahl has rightly observed that it is far more economical to rule by means of authority than by means of coercion."

Types of Authority

Power cannot be sought to be legitimized solely by the use of ideology. There must be permanent source where from the power holder may derive his legitimacy. Max Weber have identified three sources of authority such as the rational, the traditional and the charismatic source and corresponding to these sources, there may be three types of authority such as the *rational legal*, the *traditional* and the *charismatic authority*.

In case of *rational legal authority*, obedience is given to a set of impersonal orders which are inherent in an office. So here legitimacy specifically lies with the office and not on the individual actor who exercises power. As such, obedience to authority, is given not to the individual holding office, but to the legally established orders which sets out the rights and duties of the power holder.

In case of *traditional authority*, legitimacy is secured in the long established pattern of order and tradition. Here the authority lies with a person exercising power and not on any office. So the right to compliance is based on a belief of personal loyality within an area of accustomed obligation. The legitimacy, here lies with the belief in the sanctity of the settled traditions an customs of the society, so people obey a tribal chief because of this attitude only.

In case of *charismatic authority*, the feeling of obedience and the right of compliance are integrately related to a person who exercises power. The people obey a charismatic leader without questioning the validity of his orders because of his exceptional qualities which are purely personal of the power holder. People are impressed by virtue of his possession of some exceptional qualities which differentiate him from any other ordinary individual.

Max Weber observes that as charismatic authority is based on personal potentialities of the leaders, so obedience ends when the leader dies. This means a durable power relationship could not be possible in case of a charismatic authority. However, in order to establish a strong and durable power relationship, Weber argues, the charismatic authority, once established, tends to be institutionalized either in the direction of rational-legal or traditional authority. This process of getting transformed into either rational-legal or traditional type by the charismatic authority, is called by Weber, as the 'routinization of charisma." In this process the charismatic element does nor disappear rather, it became dissociated from the individual leader and embodied in the objective institutional structure.

LEGITIMACY

Legitimacy is the key concept of political power and it gives the authority only a meaning in the political system. Authority exercises the rights, sanctions, and other immunities and privileges not for authority originates in them, but owing to people's belief in the source of the bases of their rights to exercise power. The base or source of authority is called legitimacy.

Meaning & Definitions

The legitimacy, is derived from the Latin word 'legitimus' which means lawful or according to law. To action which takes place in conformity with the legal order is called legitimate action. People's consent is considered to be one of the important criteria for legitimacy. Legitimacy can be distinguished from usurpation. Usurper is a person who seizes power and tries to strengthen his position by giving his government a legitimate form. Further, even revolutions are not illegitimate because when they succeed they introduce a new principle of legitimacy which supersedes the legitimacy of the former regime. All this implies that the leaders of the political system try to cloth their actions with the concept of legitimacy.

To Max Weber, legitimacy is based on the belief of the people and it elicit obedience. Robert Dahl have given a very impressive and analytical definition of the concept of legitimacy. He said that legitimacy is the belief that the structures, procedures, acts, decisions, policies, officials or leaders of the government possess the quality of 'rightness', propriety, moral goodness and should be accepted because of this quality, irrespective of the specific content of the particular act in question."

According to Dolf Sternberger Legitimacy "is the foundation

of governmental power. It is exercised both as consciousness on part of the government that it has a right to govern and with some acknowledgement by the governed that the government has a right to do so."

Dahl is of the view that leaders in a political system always try to convert their influence into authority. Authority is the exercise of legitimate power. Legitimacy enables a ruler to govern with minimum resources. The greater is legitimacy, the lesser will be the coercion involved in governing. The willingness of the people to obey the decisions of the authority is only due to the fact that the decisions of the authority is deemed to be legitimate.

According to David Apter, legitimacy is related to a set of conceptions held by significant members of the polity about the rightness of the political pattern, which in turn, provides the pattern with a set of properties. Legitimacy is thus, a behavioural term referring to a set of limits of government action.

A distinction could be made between 'legality' and legitimacy, even though, it is very difficult to draw a sharp line of distinction between the two. The legality of a rule implies it should be according to positive law. On the otherhand, legitimacy refers to the decision taken in conformity of the wishes of the people and there by it sought people's obedience. There may be the instance of a rule which may be legal but nor legitimate.

Typology of Legitimacy

Legitimacy can be classified into two broad categories such as numinous legitimacy and civil legitimacy. Numinous legitimacy is based on the faith in the divine origin of rule. Thus here the right to obedience has a philosophical and spiritual foundation. The people obey the authority because they think the authority to be the incarnation of divinity. On the otherhand, civil legitimacy exists when the system of government is based on agreement between equally autonomous constituents. Here legitimacy flows the impersonal orders setting out rights and duties of both the govern and the governed. Thus in present day the constitution of a state, whether written or unwritten plays a vital role as the source of legitimacy. Max Weber tried to apply the concept of legitimacy to the socio-political phenomena. He asserted that in a legitimate dominion of any type, legitimacy is based on belief of the people and it elicit obedience. He refers to three types of legitimacy as rational legal, traditional and charismatic. By rational legitimacy, Weber implies the belief in the legal pattern of normative rules and the rights of those elevated to the authority under such rules to issue commands. So rational legal legitimacy is inextricably related to an office issuing command. By traditional legitimacy, Max Weber means the patriarchal and feudal forms of dominion.

By charismatic legitimacy, Weber means the uniqueness of the prophets, heroes and other leaders who issue commands. Here the belief of the people is based on the exceptional personality of the person exercising authority.

Friedrich says five types of legitimacy such as religious, philosophical, traditional, procedural and pragmatic. The concept of religious legitimacy go back to the times of ancient empire when the king was considered as the son of god and obedience to him was not only a political necessity but also politically expedient. This may be considered as the modern notion of numinous legitimacy.

Sources of Legitimacy

The source of legitimacy vary from person to person. Weber classified three sources of legitimacy such as the traditional, charismatic and rational-legal source. Besides Max Weber such typology of sources, the need and feeling for justice can also be regarded as a source of legitimacy. In fact, the ideology of the people, and not of the rulers, is the main source of legitimacy.

Legitimacy is not a high level abstract thinking but a phenomena existing underlying the whole system. It is related to the whole system and its governance. It is not a moral feeling or subjective conceptualization. It is a belief of the people in the rightness of the activities of the government. In Easton's view, legitimacy relates to the authoritative allocation of values in the society.

It is legitimacy which enables the political actors to transform influence into authority. In the context of third world countries, legitimacy plays a key role in running their political systems. Within the bounds of legitimacy, political leaders, parties, groups and individuals are allowed to compete among themselves.

Legitimacy, in the context of political system means public or political accountability. As all citizens have a faith in the legitimacy of its structures, procedures and functioning its responsibility to operate within its confines or 'rightness' increases manifold, so as to respond to their hopes and expectations. These expectations must be accomplished more with the exercise of influence, authority and leadership than force, coercion and violence. Authorities do have right to exercise force, domination, manipulation and other sanctions, but their use should strictly confine dispassionately to the accepted of legitimacy, the exercise of power of force cannot be treated as coercion or violence. An legitimate Authority bestows right to issue orders and directives, take decisions. Make policies and run administration through various agencies, subject to higher rational principles of social life.

It should be noted that legitimacy does not always mean blind obedience to laws or decisions in spite of the belief in the authority, people can oppose or support them for their instrumental losses or gains and the former can persist even by allowing them to pursue their own goals. However, it has to accommodate such demands for strengthening itself as it feels necessary to be.

LEADERSHIP

The concept of power, rule and authority have very often been related with the concept of leadership. Leadership is often characterized as a quality of communication. Its place is becoming more and more prominent because of the divergence of human activities and the expansion of the activities of state. It acts as the search light and the steering wheel of a vehicle.

Dimensions of Leadership

Leadership has a variety of dimensions. In the social aspect, leadership refers to those people in the society who guides the activates of group. These leaders have the controlling power and thereby they exercise a great deal of influence nor only over the individual followers but also over the issue areas of public concern. In the economic sphere, leadership refers to the owners of business firms and those people who have an easy access to the process of distribution, control and exchange of the production. In the field of politics, leadership refers to the public servants and statesmen as well as the politicians who have undertaken the task of providing guideline to the masses. It thus refers to the elite groups in the society. In the matter of public administration, leadership refers to the process of management of organizations. It is a process of getting things done with the help of others on the line of cooperation.

Meaning

Leadership is not a new social phenomena. It was present in the society since it came into existence. As James Lundy observes, "Leadership essentially involves the task of planning, coordinating, motivating and controlling the efforts of others towards a specific objective."

Ordway Tead observes that "leadership is the activity of influencing people to cooperate with some goals which they come to find as desirable.

A leader is a person who leads the group or an organization or a nation towards a definite set of objectives. This means that a leader is always ahead of the term inmates which it has been leading. In other words, leadership signifies the place of a person who commands obedience, respect and who is obeyed and followed by the subordinates. Leadership does not want to concentrate powers in its own hand, but power automatically flows to him due to his caliber, efficiency and behaviour.

H. Koontz and G.O'Donnel defines leadership as the activity of persuading people to cooperate in the achievement of common objectives."

Bernard says, "leadership refers to the quality of behaviour of individuals where by they guide people of their activities in organized efforts. While Britt says, " Leadership is the process of mutual stimulation or reciprocal reinforcement which controls the human energy in the pursuit of a common goal."

The above definitional aspects of leadership highlight the fact leadership cannot operate in a vacuum. This means there are certain factors which influence leadership. In other words leadership is situational. There can be no leader without somebody to lead. Followers are also vital to leadership. Leaders come into being as a result of common consent of people who, then willingly become followers. Thus real leaders come into being through the voluntary acknowledgement of those being led. Besides, time and circumstances are important moulders of leadership. Most leaders are conditioned by the time in which they live and the particular set of circumstances with which they were all confronted with and in which they operated. This is called the situational interpretation of leadership.

Undoubtedly, both interpretations are partially right because the most memorable leaders have had the ability to unify and motivate the people to achieve important goals. It is also true that one of the reasons these leaders are remembered is that they operated during critical moments in history.

Leadership Traits

A leader is not an ordinary member of the policy. He possesses certain characteristics by virtue of which he may be able to lead and guide the people. Different scholars have their own interpretation about leadership traits which is expected in a leader. Bernard narrated four essential characteristics of leaders such as vitality, decisiveness, power of endurance and foresight and capacity to persuade others. With the help of these traits, a leader always goes on controlling and directing the masses.

Millet enlists the following characteristics of a leader such as good health, sense of mission, interest in fellow beings, intellectual capability, high intelligent quotient, persuasiveness, judgment of good and bad and loyalty.

According to Prof. G.R. Terry, energy, emotional stability, knowledge of human relations, personal motivation, communication skill, teaching ability, social skill and technical competence etc. are some of the traits which every leader have to follow in one way or the other.

With the help of the above said traits, the leaders always try to solve the issues of public concern. The type of leadership in any society is always influenced by its socio-political environment. Still, higher education also plays a significant role in leadership traits. The elite theorist identify leaders with the elites and says that the elites provide the leadership because of their organized minority. They have also the qualities of both fox and lion, says Pareto.

Types of Leadership

Many attempts have been made by different scholars to have a clear typology of leadership on the basis of different criteria of classification. The classification of Max Weber is most note worthy and also highly satisfactory. Weber was of the opinion that the stability of a society depends on the right of the leaders to exercise power and at the same time, the acceptance of the formal authority of the leaders by the general masses. He classified three types of leadership such as the charismatic, the traditional and the bureaucratic.

In traditional leadership, the leaders rule the society by virtue of birth or social position in the society. The leader gains authority from traditional customs and practices. The authority of ruling was granted to the leader because the people have a faith in the long established customs and traditions. This implies that the traditional leadership is always ascriptive in nature.

Bureaucratic officials make another category whose authority is based on the written rules. It implies that these are the rational legal leaders who possesses some technical competence. These are the people who are highly intelligent, decisive and prompt decision makers. These leaders always work on principles and thereby able to guide the people in the society. They are capable men having far reaching foresights. Obedience is given to such leaders not because of their personal qualities but because of the follower's faith in the office of the leaders, based on impersonal rules and orders.

In actual practice leadership can be conveniently classified into the following nine categories: 1) personal 2) Non-personal; 3) authoritatian; 4) democratic 5) paternalistic; 6) indigenous 7) conservative; 8) radical leadership; and 9) liberal leadership.

Leadership Styles

Leadership style is inextricably related with leader's ultimate success or failure. Leadership style is often defined as the consistent behaviour pattern of the leader through which he handles the various situations and crises. Although a wide variety of leadership style exists, and any style may be successful when applied at the right time and place, yet over the years, a categorization of styles have developed. The most common and the longest acceptable differentiation is between the authoritarian and democratic leadership styles.

Democratic leaders are interested in the masses and recognize their individuality. They accept the people's participation in decision making process through tacit selection. They are willing to accept and consider the ideas and suggestions presented to them by the members of the society on any social or political issue. They allow maximum independence and flexibility in the society.

Authoritarian leaders do not identify themselves as the members of a cohesive group. The leaders dominate coercian to comply with their orders. Thus the leaders do not integrate themselves as a member of the society rather they want to maintain a distance from the masses. The main objective of the leaders were to get their orders done by the masses. The leaders are arbitrary in nature and thus they do not wish to share the ideas. Suggestions never welcomed by the leaders from the masses.

However, equally important is the ability of the leader to maintain his position and powers in the society. Thus leadership must consider not only the motivational aspects but also should concentrate on other equal aspects like decision making, planning, controlling, communicating etc.

3

Concept of International Community

The nation state embodies an implicit assumption that the constituent part of the state, the individual human being, is a 'political animal' pure and simple. Man as citizen is considered to have no interests of motivations other than those that arise from his membership in a political group, and he is supposed to discover complete personal fulfilment in the performance of his civic duties.

The fact of human nature, however, run contrary to this operating hypothesis of statesmen. Despite the great increase in the functions of government, there remains a vast area of individual activity that is 'non-political': that is, it is either untouched by the state or else governmental intervention is unhappy or unsuccessful. Men simply cannot, despite the efforts of the most totalitarian of dictators, live all their lives within the arms of the state. Growing out of this failure of political authority to achieve true totality and as a result of the greater impetus. Provided by the expanding technology of our time, more and more individuals have had their lives touched by other individuals from different states.

Although by no means of equal effect in every case, this increase in private international relationships has served in some measure to diminish the more extreme effects of nationalist bias in many people.

This effect has not been ignored by governments. Those that have had the greatest interest in the perpetuation of intense nationalist rivalry have been most active in attempting to reduce the frequency of private international contacts.

The government of the USSR, whose principal domestic propaganda line has been to insist that the Russian peoples have nothing in common with those of the capitalist world, has been the worst offender in this regard, closely followed by the government of Communist China.

Despite the cold war and other restrictive policies of governments, private international relationships have been expanding and have grown to the point where they perceptibly affect the political relations of states. As people representing different states and cultures come into contact in pursuit of common objectives, they frequently discover that the cultural then Furnaces between them become less glaring and their common humanity group in importance.

These groups are both governmental and private some have lofty objectives, while others are more pedestrian in their good. They all share one common characteristic: they provide basis upon which men of differing political allegiance can co-operate in the attainment of shared objective that so important to each of them.

While an individual is involved in such an activity, he cannot escape undergoing a basic readjustment in his political outlook. He can no longer think of foreign states as corporate entities or political abstractions; Great Britain, France, of Japan ceases to be monolithic structure but instead is thought of as a collection of individual human beings very much like himself.

His acquaintance with particular Britons or Japanese and the relations he has with them serve to modify his point of view of the political group of which they are a part.

Private International Relationships

It is one of the many paradoxes of modern political life that the present day, in which the role of the state and the compelling force of nationalism have grown to the zenith in history, has at the same time witnessed the greatest multiplication of private international relationships. As citizens, men are urged on every side to forsake all international identification and to adhere only to their state and to their own national group.

In their private lives, however, more and more of them have experienced some form of personal contact with other peoples. This, to many, serves to make the conflict between private interest and public (national) interest more real and more poignant.

The trend at the present time is unquestionably in the direction of a continued intensification in the conflict, because governments today are not yet ready to relax much of their grip upon the loyalties of men.

At the same time, more and more individuals everywhere are being caught up in the ever-expanding network of private relationships that reach across frontiers. Before proceeding to an analysis of the international-community sense and compact upon world politics, it is necessary to examine a few of the factors the help to explain the great increase in these contacts.

Revolution of Transportation and Communication

The principal reason for the increase in international contact is the fact that the world has grown smaller. Modern devices of transportation and communication have made any part of the world immediately accessible by radio, telephone, or wireless communication, while no portion of the globe is more than a few hours away from any other point by rapid air transportation.

A good deal of what has been written and said about man's conquest of space and time either has been hackneyed and platitudinous or else has ignored its broader implications for civilization. Nevertheless, the facts are clear for all to see: many people have taken immediate advantage of these rapid and relatively inexpensive methods of broadening their personal horizons. All areas of human social life are affected by these devices.

Economic life has been greatly modified and the social, religious, and recreational activities of individuals in most of the world have been revolutionized by the radio and the airplane.

Transportation. Rapid *transportation* is so much a commonplace or contemporary life in Western society that most of us realize only vaguely how it has changed the very tempo of our civilization. Today the airplane has revolutionized concepts of distance. In 1952 the British Overseas Aircraft Company placed in service the first scheduled jet passenger airliner; its elapsed.

To cross the Atlantic in the eighteenth century required weeks of uncomfortable and dangerous sailing; today modern steamship make the crossing in less than four days and aircraft in only twelve hours.

Thus, London is closer to New York today than Philadelphia was at the time of the Revolution.

Since the construction of hard-surfaced highways, the privately owned automobile has also worked major changes in the range of mobility of individuals.

The means that, granted the curiosity of the human species, more and more individuals will take advantage of the opportunity to travel—for whatever reason—as facilities are improved. Statistics confirm this hypothesis.

This constant increase in the employment of air facilities for the international travel means that more people are crossing frontiers by air at the time and in the consummation of their business are making the personnel contact and are receiving the impressions that are inevitable.

Communication. With introduction of cellular phone, which has become a plaything even in developing countries, communication has become most easy. There are a number of means to communicate message viz. e-mail, SMS, Fax etc. Anyone within reach of a telephone can speak with any other part of the world within a few moments, and technical improvements are being made steadily.

There are more than 75 million telephone instruments in the world, scattered over all continents and in most countries, all tied together into one vast network. International telegraphs and cable facilities provide another means of rapid communication.

By these devices personal communication between individuals becomes extremely easy and rapid; international postal service by air has served again to reduce drastically the time required to exchange more detailed communication by letter mail. Of equal, although different, significance is the great expansion of the devices of mass, as opposed to individual, communication. The most important of these are the radio and the motion pictures.

Radio waves know no frontier, and particularly in Europe, where the political units are so small, any regular radio listener is offered a broad international menu of programmes to suit his taste. Even in the United States, home radio receivers have become of powerful that to receive broadcasts from Europe, South America, or even Asia is a common place for millions of Americans.

In 1954, there were approximately 240 radio receivers in use throughout the world, of which 130 million were in the United States and 67 million in Europe. This obviously represents an enormous audience for broadcasting, the internationalizing effect of which is easy to imagine.

Motion pictures also exert a great influence upon the international attitudes of people everywhere. Latest estimates are that there are throughout the world nearly 1,00,000 motion-picture theatres with a total seating capacity of over 43 million.

The American motion-picture industry has played the leading role in the internationalization of the film. American-made productions go all over the world, into Europe and Asia and Africa, carrying with them their message of the American way of life; revenue from foreign bookings bulks large in the calculations of American producers.

Lately, the process has been somewhat reversed; films are being made in foreign locations by American companies (largely because of restrictions upon currency exchange) and thus American audiences are furnished visual demonstration of the physical and human backgrounds of foreign countries, all without ever leaving home.

The international movement of motion pictures has been made more nearly mutual since World War II as British, French, Italian, German, and some Japanese films have obtained mass audiences in the United States.

We are not arguing that improved transportation and communications are themselves necessarily conducive to greater international understanding. It is clearly easier today for many people to establish contact with individuals in other states and more and more people are doing so. Whether this is for good or ill depends upon the circumstances of the particular relationship.

Economic Interdependence

Despite the efforts of certain governments in recent years to achieve economic self-sufficiency, the various parts of the world stand in a relation of economic interdependence if the resources of modern industrial production are to be exploited to their maximum advantage for all individuals everywhere. In the face of much political control of international economic life, trade reflecting these mutual needs continues to move; in the process, individuals follow their commerce.

No relationship is more universally human than that of buying and selling; in the conduct of international trade some of the closest and most lasting international private relationships are created.

Some of the principal participants in world politics must import many more vital commodities than does the United States. Great Britain, for example, imports approximately half of its basic foodstuffs, including meat and cereals; France must normally import the great bulk of is coal; Italy must import both coal and iron ore, in addition to a large amount of food.

The more one examines the structure of world economic relationships; the more the lesson of the economic interdependence of peoples is borne home.

Politicians may seek, for good reasons or ill, to create self-sufficient enclaves within the borders of their states, but at best this is extremely difficult and possible only at the cost of serious dislocations in the lives of private citizens.

It is a fact of contemporary politics in many parts of the world—especially western Europe—that individuals are growing increasingly doubtful of the wisdom of choosing nationalist autarky over the improved standard of living possible through international economic co-operation.

The Benelux Customs Unio and the Schumann Plan are only two of the many items of evidence that emphasize the force of this sentiment.

Opening of Underdeveloped Areas

The Underdeveloped Areas. Closely allied to the general situation of the economic interdependence of peoples as a factor in the augmentation of international private contacts is the special case of the recent opening of the underdeveloped areas of the world to modern techniques.

In Asia, Africa, the Middle East, and Latin America, the period since 1945 has witnessed the initiation of extensive two-way contact and communication between these great portions of the world and Western civilization.

Before World War II, the areas that we today term "underdeveloped" presented certain common characteristics which have affected the role of their peoples in contemporary life.

In the first place, most of them were resented from the mainstream of either private or public international life; they were largely unaware of what went on outside their boundaries, and the remainder of the world to a great extent reciprocated this ignorance. Secondly, either they were all colonies of imperialist state or, although technically independent, they had never economically or politically emerged from a colonial orientation; that is, nationalist self-consciousness was only imperfectly developed and self-government was either nonexistent or very ineffective.

Third, they uniformly possessed low standard of living and made only extremely inefficient use of their natural and human resource endowment. Social and economic discontent, although usually submerged, was widespread because of flagrant inequities in the distributions of the rewards of the society.

Since the end of the war these areas have all erupted. Politically and economically they have suddenly broken out into the main stream of world affairs and have attempted each in its own way, to initiate an attack upon the world political community had suddenly increased its membership by some two dozen states. The 'underdeveloped' peoples refuse to be taken for granted any more and their impact upon international life is already great and will continue to grow.

Problems of political, economic, and racial adjustment have pressed upon us simultaneously with the obligation to gain some sort of factual education about what sort of people these are. We have also had to devise techniques for teaching them about ourselves, which has proved to be difficult. Most of our historical contacts with foreigners have been with Europeans, whose value systems and cultural backgrounds spring from the same roots as do our own. Copping with states such as India and Indonesia, Iran and Egypt, all of whom have revolted against Western imperialism, has forced us to re-examine many of our own assumptions in order to discover that approach which will procure a sympathetic hearing for our own case.

For the moment let us look at certain concrete ways in which their entry into the world has increased in individual contacts between their propels and the individual citizens of other states.

Political Contacts. In the political field, the fact that almost all these states are now executing their own foreign policies with near-belligerent independence has in itself increased their impact upon the rest of the world. India, Pakistan, Burma, the Philippines, and many other similar states now for the first time maintain diplomatic relations with most of the other governments in the world.

Natives of these states thus come into direct contact with the governmental machinery and the cultural flow of all Western states, with an in companying acceleration in the education of all concerned.

This effect is tightened by the fact that the diplomats of the new states are all drawn from the leadership class in their homelands and exert an influence out of proportion to their small numbers.

The process of acculturation also works in reverse. Foreign states maintain diplomatic establishments in each of the new states and the citizens of the younger governments come into contact with official representatives of many cultures of which they had previously been only vaguely aware. In like manner actively in the United Nations has served to speed up this getting-acquainted process in a unique manner; the participation in the Korean war of military contingents from such exotic states as Thailand and Turkey served to bring the peculiar contributions of these peoples to the attention of the world better than any other single action they have taken.

The industrialized West must accept the fact of an independent East that is determined to be treated as an equal, but so must the new states rid themselves of some of their most deep-seated and erroneous antipathies toward Western civilization.

Economic Contacts. It is in the area of economic life that the underdeveloped areas and the Western world have come into the closest and most intimate contact. Before 1941, the economic resources of these territories were, generally speaking, under the direct exploitation of western capitalists; since then, the inhabitants have to a considerable degree taken over the determination of their own economic destinies.

This has been an enlightening experience for everyone concerned. The problems of production, transportation, and distribution of the commodities produced and their exchange for other products in the markets of the world have proved both more complicated and more simple than originally imagined.

Technical knowledge of production is often lacking among these peoples, as is also experience in marketing and distributing the goods produced.

The outside world has had in turn to learn the peculiar way of doing business followed by the relatively inexperienced representatives of these areas. The Western world and the underdeveloped areas are coming into wider economic contact than ever before and each has a great deal to learn from the others. It has not been a process altogether easy and happy, but it has been a necessary one that promises to continue for a long time.

The programme of technical assistance and co-operation with the underdeveloped areas undertaken by the United States—known as Point IV' from its inclusion as the last point in a four-part American foreign policy by President Truman in 1949—is perhaps the most ambitious and well-tensioned policy followed by any Western government in dealing with the new states. It is based upon the unquestioned need of these areas for the kind of technical economic assistance that only the West can provide. It proceeds upon a completely voluntary on the part of the state requesting the assistance, and includes primarily the furnishing of private investment capital from the United States and the supplying of technically trained experts in various fields to serve the needs of the host country.

In the course of its execution, American technicians have aided agriculture in India, mines in Burma, and public health in Thailand as well as many other similar projects. Many people regard the programme as especially hopeful because of its practical application. Instead of involving intergovermental relationship at a high level, it actually represents individuals engaged in extending a helping hand to other individuals in an attack upon problems that are highly personnel in their impact.

Some of the greatest failures of the programme have come as a result of attempts to impose an American procedure upon a situation completely unsuitable for it; likewise, its greatest successes have accompanied a realization that an agricultural problem in India, for example, may be solved only by the gradual application of Western techniques to a situation that is and will remain—uniquely Indian.

This of necessity has required the modification of many Western techniques of organization, efficiency, and production in order to fit them within the bounds of a differing value structure.

Other Individual Contacts

The main cause, however, for the increasing amount of individual international contact is the movement of unorganized private citizens in the pursuit of their individual interests. In the part of world which is still sufficiently free to permit reasonably easy movement buy private individuals across frontiers, there is a constant two-way traffic.

Education. International education is an old custom, especially in the Western world. Since the Middle Ages it has been normal for students to seek the completion of their formal education in foreign institutions. This, however, was largely confined to Europe, where a common culture existed of which the universities were among the principal custodians.

The United States plays a leading role in this process. As a matter of policy the American government emphasizes private international contact through education, feeling that in this important area real progress can be made onwards minimizing inter cultural tension. It operates an international educational exchange programme whereby foreign students and professors from all over the world may come to the United States to study or teach; in 1953-54 there were over 30,000 such visitors in American institutions of higher learning.

At the same time many-sided programme undertakes to make study broad available to American students. The largest single such group are the Fluorite scholars, Approximately 600 per year, who study in any of some nineteen states in Europe or Asia.

They enjoy scholarships provided by the unexpended accounts remaining from United States lend-lease operations during World War II. Similar opportunities exist for American professors, both to teach and to do research abroad, under the Fluorite programme.

There are many privately financed international fellowships and the Ford Foundation fellowships for study in the Middle and Far East.

All in all, the programme of American campuses, even small campuses, are commonplace; Americans abroad are an equally familiar phenomenon.

These are residence and social centres for foreign students. In this way students from abroad not only learn about the United States, but acquire much sophistication from the intimate contact with other foreign students.

Thus an Indian student in the United States may have a Brazilian as a room-mate. In this way the process of student acculturation gains a new dimension. Education an exchange between Europe and the Orient.

It is particularly important that the lessons of common humanity and sympathetic understanding be taught within the college and university community in all states because it is from this group that the leaders of the future will come.

The attitude toward other peoples held by the current generation of college students in the United States can never be the same as a result of its contact with so many foreign students.

Recreation. The pursuit of recreation leads many individuals into international set, which journeyed from one famous recreational playground and another, but its importance was never great and today is negligible. Of much more importance is organized international athletic competition. The most publicized event of this sort is of course the quadrennial Olympic games, in which athletes from all over the world compete in many different events. But it would be difficult to mention a form of athletics, either professional or amateur, which does not extend into the international arena. Team sports, such as soccer, football, basketball, baseball, water polo, and hockey have regularly scheduled incantational tournaments; in addition, national champions in these and other sports make international tours as a matter of course.

A noteworthy example of international athletic competition is the annual pursuit of the Davis Cup, for which national teams of tennis players compete in a world-wide tournament. Individual sports—tennis, golf, boxing, wrestling, weight lifting, tract and field, and the like—also provide innumerable opportunities for international competition. Indeed, so systematized in international athletic competition that almost any athlete of sufficient talent, regardless of his particular speciality, can look forward to the opportunity of performing in foreign land and in competition with opponents of different nationalities.

Despite the Soviet government's desire to make political capital out of the competition and the unfavourable atmosphere of Russo-American relations at the time, American team members reported to the press that they found their Russian opponents to be very pleasant individuals and sturdy competitors. What the Russian athletes told their government we have no way of knowing.

Tourism. Perhaps the most prolific source of personal international experiences, at least for Americans, is tourism. Since the war American tourists and travellers have come to include the entire globe in their itinerary, taken great advantage of the growth of air transportation.

The United States government has encouraged this practice for two reasons. In the first place tourist expenditures represent a very considerable transfer of dollars into foreign hands, making it easier for them to purchase American goods. In the second, tourism, being travel for no ulterior purpose, provides an ideal opportunity for Americans to learn about the ways of life in foreign countries.

As a rest tourism by Americans has grown to remarkable proportions and the American who has `been abroad' is no longer a local curiosity throughout each of the United States.

Europeans are almost as great travellers as are Americans and, despite currency and travel restrictions, have covered much of the Western world with their wanderings.

In Asia, the smallness of the leisure class and the great distances to be traversed have made travel by Asians less common; however, much of non-communist Asia is regularly visited by tourists from the West and some international contact thus takes place.

The Effects of World War II. Although in no sense pleasant and in most cases involuntary, there was, as an inescapable concomitant of the war and its aftermath, a great increase in the number and the variety of private international relationships.

Hostile occupation, the forcible transfer of workers, prisoners of war, displaced persons, refugees, and military comradeship all produced mass international contacts among private persons upon a scale unmatched at any time before or since.

Its effects are still being felt. Many Frenchmen perceived, even in the bitterness of defeat, that the Germans are human beings and the most of them are human beings and that most of them are decent; Germans learned the same about the French.

The Japanese, at first despised and then hysterically hated by Americans, turned out on closer acquaintance to be human beings who have the same sort of personal problems as we do but who solve them somewhat differently. Even the Soviet Union felt the impact.

The hundreds of thousands of Red Army soldiers who saw the West with their won eyes in Germany and Austria, as well as the Russian slave labourers. Hitler forcibly deported to the West during the war, will never again have the same degree of trust in the Kremlin's propaganda about the decayed and dying West.

In this way the world reaped an unexpected harvest of good from the war. The sheer volume of personal contact that developed, ranging from casual acquaintanceship to international marriages, has worked and will continue to work a fundamental change in the outlook of millions of people.

The International Sense of Community

The term "community" is defined by sociologists in a number of different ways, but all the definitions include certain common features. There are four essential aspects of a community. First, it is composed of individuals who may or may not be organized into subgroups. Second, these individuals have extensive and habitual relations with one another which are sufficiently well organized to proceed upon a highly predictable basis. Third, there exists within the group a generally recognized moral consensus that establishes the value system in whose terms certain are demanded by the community, others encouraged or permitted, and the others prohibited. Fourth, the habitual relations of the individuals and the value system are both reflected in a framework of institutions.

The International Community Sense

The international sense of community consists in the realization shared by an increasing number of individuals in almost all state of the world that they form part of a group which processes most of the marks of a true community. This community bypasses political organization and political action. Its focus of emphasis is upon the rough identity of interest shared by its members in their private lives. In terms of the criteria of a communist which we listed above, the international community displays the following characteristics.

1. Its members are generally organized into subgroups (private and public international organization), but whether within or without such a subgroup, extensive and habitual personal relations are carried on.
2. These are developing certain procedural patterns and organization, and predictability in these relationship is developing rapidly.
3. The moral consensus that marks a true community is still in the process of maturation, but its outlines are already clear. It is individual in its emphasis and places primary value upon the dignity of the human being.
4. To enforce its value judgments the international community is developing a set of sanctions, most of them thus far informal, to prescribe desirable behaviour and to punish antisocial conduct.
5. Extensive institutional elaboration of this community

sense has already taken place land the process in continuing to day at the ever-increasing rate.

Nationalism and Technology: Since the creation of the nation-state system about six centuries ago, the largest political unit reflecting the sense of community shared by its members has been the nation state. The state had to win its victory over other, smaller community units for the prize of the loyalty of its people.

The history of the development of the state in modern times can be told in terms of the expansion of the community sense of the people until it actually encompassed the entire national group. Two forces played critical roles in this process.

The first was the development of *modern nationalism,* which identified the body of citizens with the effective community; the second was *modern technology* which made the pretensions of nationalism a reality by making it possible for all people within a state to maintain close and habitual relations with all the others.

Nationalism in most societies today however more sharp distinctions between the in-group and all out-groups, and demonstrates an increasing proclivity toward ethnocentric excesses; on the other hand, the advance of modern technology did not come to a halt at the frontiers of the national state but instead leaped over them.

The technological frontier now extends to the outermost limits of the entire world. It is an easy matter for individuals to maintain `extensive relations' upon an organized basis with people in all other states.

In many ways the cruel dilemma of modern man is the result of the contemporary conflict between these two formerly harmonious forces. Nationalism bids him to confine his loyalty and his effective action to the members of his own particular group; technology provides him a world-wide arena for action, with possibilities for good which at present are only hinted at.

The international-community sense is most conspicuous among those individuals everywhere who have accepted the implications of global technology and who have therefore won freedom from the more limited points of view imposed by the more restrictive variety of nationalism.

Components of the International-Community Sense

If the international-community sense is defined as an attitude shared by large numbers of individuals throughout the world, it now becomes appropriate to consider its component parts. Individuals vary in their understanding of what membership in the international community means; many persons pursue an active part in the affairs of the community without realizing the assumptions upon which they are proceeding.

Individualism: In the first place, the international-community sense is individualistic in its outlook. It rejects the totalitarian implications of the dogma of the modern state and denies that men have no higher destiny than to serve their governments in all ways that political leadership deems to befitting. It clearly involves an elevation of the claims of the individual to dignity and worthy over the pretensions of the state to absolute dominance.

Being essentially a philosophy of individualism it is identified with the classic theory of natural rights and limited government, which is also a part of the democratic concept.

Since in international affairs the state is everything and the individual has no legal existence, the international-community sense rejects much of international law and almost all of what we know as 'power politics.'

It is a philosophy if international affairs which centres upon the individual human being instead of upon the abstract entity of the state. In this sense it is more realistic than nationalistic particulars since the individual has objective reality and the state and the national do not.

It may seem paradoxical that an outlook which emphasizes the prime importance of the individual should seek the broadest possible base of organization. If the state today results in the abasement of a individual, it might be thought odd to urge the creation of a new community to include of mankind; to change from a large group to one still larger in the name of more dignity and freedom for the individual is a seeming contradiction. But they must remember the influence of technology.

The state form of organization, say the apologists for the international community, obstructs the most efficient use of the technological resources of the world in terms of the maximum benefit for individuals; the economies of large-scale production can be federalized by utilizing all mankind in a single body of producers and consumers. Technology leads us to the world community and the greater freedom and dignity of man.

Anti-Sadism: The international-community sense not only denies the pre-eminence of the state over the individual; its outlook is primarily non-political. Instead of being concerned with problems of national interest, national power, and national prestige, it makes a special point of the highly personal problems of individuals in the economic, social, and psychological areas. It seems to argue that although man unquestionably is a political being, he is first and always a human; as such, he is beset from birth with a host of situations that strike him much more directly than even the most fervent pleas of political authority.

He must find food and shelter; he must marry and establish a family; he must combat disease; he must gain enough knowledge of socially useful skills to enable him to cope with the world; he must learn the formal and informal rules of social organization so that he can fit himself meaningful into the group of which he is a part.

The international-community sense synthesis upon these aspects of the lives of individuals and seeks to discover some of the solutions to these personal problems. It elevates the private life of man over the political life, and views government as one of the possible vehicles for the enrichment and fulfilment of the life of individuals rather than as the embodiment of the life of individuals rather than as the embodiment of the supremacy of the political virtues.

It accordingly expects from government in the international field a different role from that played by the states of today, it demands cooperative attack by political authority upon the problems of men rather than the competitive pursuit of national interest.

The Identity of Individual Interest: The idea of the international community is founded upon the basic identity of interest among all individuals. Building upon the sociological and anthropological truth of essential similarity of all people and the fact that cultural and societal differences between men is learned rather than innate, the international-community sense assumes fail all men share basically the same needs and desires. Whatever in the way of governmental policy anywhere serves to improve the lot of individuals is deemed desirable; whatever serves any other purpose is held to be of secondary importance. This means that the shares of the sense of international community reject cost of the nationalist apparatus of modern international politics on the ground that it creates a false disharmony of interest between individuals of different national groups.

Of course, the identity of individual interest of which so much is made in this argument refers to the basic humanity of individuals. Nationalisms be founded upon false premises; ideologies may be over simplification of what may be at best only half-truths; cultural differences may be learned and therefore synthetic.

All these divisive forces of modern world life, however, are real and powerful in their effect upon human emotions, and to seek to offset them by attempts at scientific refutation is a waste of time. The only way in which an individual who denies his identity of interest with all other men can be brought to change his mind is for him to be placed in situations of direct contact with representatives of alien cultures.

Once brought face to face with the obvious fact that these strangers must cope with the same sort of problems as he does, the psychological underpinnings of his faith in his own uniqueness are weakened.

Once enough individuals had gained the sophistication in outlook that made it possible for them to grasp the important fact of the essential sameness of human everywhere, the concept of international community became a potent force in world affairs.

Loss of Faith in State Mechanism: As a result of the defect of technology, many men everywhere have developed doubts about the ultimate validity of political values. They wonder whether the demands that international politics make upon individuals return rewards that are worth what they cost and whether the fate of men is to remain forever divided into mutually competitive groups. Consequently they no longer have may confidence that the international political system, founded upon the sovereignty of the state and operating upon the principles of power and of expediency, can every produce any lasting improvement of human happiness. Theirs is not simply a theory of philosophic anarchy hoping for a day of brotherhood that will make political organization unnecessary. The advocates of the international community seek to keep their policy practice and realistic.

They have no rigid formula for action except in terms, of the eventual recognition of the equal right of all individuals to a reasonably adequate satisfaction of their basic needs. Therefore, although distrusting the nation-state and the system of world politics as presently constituted and motivated, they do not necessarily call for its outright rejection.

For various people, the doubt about the personal rewards derived from state-centred international politics has not yet matured into recognition and an acceptance of the international community.

They are disillusioned about the future of men under the nation-state system, but are unable to make the transfer of allegiance to a broader basis of identification.

Nationalism, cultural isolationism, and the pressures of ideologies furnish too great an emotional obstacle for them to overcome.

Lacking confidence in the value systems of current world politics and unable to accept the activist implications of the international community, they tend to take refuge in an attempted withdrawal from political currents and use an effect cynicism at a shield against the necessity of making any meaningful choices among political alternatives.

A Programme of Action: Of course, individuals vary in the extent of their commitment in this regard as well as in the kind and extent of specific actions they undertake, but so many are the problems to be solved and so compelling is felt to be the need for their solution that purposeful activity on behalf of the goals of the community is a constant characteristic of one who feels himself a part of it.

Most often this is done through one or another of the hundreds of private international organizations. Most of these organizations, being highly specialized, accomplish comparatively little except in the area of their particular interest; many of them seem quite remote from the subject of world peace. Yet in the aggregate their impact is great.

Mention must also be made of the vast number of individuals who, with in benefit of organizational support and completely upon their own, carry of the work of the international community within the scope of their own private lives.

The total effect of thousand of such persons carrying on their programmes of agitation, education, and action over a period of years cannot leap but make a real impression upon the consciousness of governments anywhere.

The action programme on behalf of the international community operate through the state. Governments today are potentially capable of working great improvement in the lives of individuals through cooperative international effort; all that is lacking is the will to do so on the part of contemporary leadership.

Consequently, individuals interested in the advancement of the international community have banded into pressure groups in order to stimulate governmental action in that direction.

The steps taken by governments in this field include the creation and operation of special-purpose international organizations, the furthering of the social and economic work of the United Nations, and the initiation of maltreat policies of relief and rehabilitation of individuals in other states.

No doubt, that governments often have mixed motives in their operations in this field; some of them have a direct national interest in the development of a real international community sense and co-operate much more willingly than do others whose policy is founded upon a perpetuation of the national differences that divide human race.

In almost every instance, the effective implementation of any such governmental policy necessitates the unremitting application of pressure by individuals and groups who subscribe to the policy themselves to the point of becoming political activists in its support.

International Organizations: Private

Organization and Structure: A private international organization is composed of private persons who join together upon an international basis either for the direct accomplishment of an end they have in common or else to bring pressure upon their respective governments to initiate policy in harmony with their objectives.

There are many such organisations in existence at the present time, with a bewildering variety of stated purposes. They belong to either the figurative type, being composed of a number of suborganizations set up upon a national basis, or else to the consolidated type, which is truly international with no organizational apparatus intervening between the individual member and the leadership of the entire group. The most important of them have certain structural features in common. They all have a central headquarters under the direction of a chief executive officer (CEO) who normally serves as spokesman for the organization, together with some form of regularly scheduled conference of the entire membership at their representatives, at which general policy is made for the organization.

1. *Economic Purposes*: No doubt, the largest category of private international organizations is furnished by those whose objectives are the economic betterment of the individual members. At least three major sub classifications can be discerned.

Manufacturing and trade organizations include perhaps the most influential single private international organization, the International Chamber of Commerce. Other typical examples are the International Carriage and Van Union, the International Fiscal Association, the International Federation of Newspaper Publishers and Editors and the International Union of Architects. Labour organizations include the three most powerful international labour groups: the International Confederation of Port Trade Unions, the World Federation of Trade Unions, and the International Federation of Christian Trade Unions.

2. *Political Purposes*: Private international organizations with a political orientation are of two different types: they are composed either of governmental officials from various states with common problems who consult together for the more efficient accomplishment of their mission, or else of private citizens whose major function is the dissemination of information and the bringing of pressure upon their respective home governments. The first type, composed of similarly situated government officials of various

states, includes the most important of this entire category, the Inter-Parliamentary Union, whose membership is made up of legislators from many states.

Pressure and propaganda organizations include the World Federation of United Nations Associations, the International Federation for Housing and Town-Planning, the International League for the Rights of Man, and the International Union of Socialist Youth. Almost all private international organizations have a pressure-propaganda aspect as part of their programme, but those given above are some for which it is the principal function.

3. *Religious Purposes*: Religious organizations upon an international basis are numerous, representing most of the organized faith of the Western World. The Salvation Army, the World Jewish Congress, the Young Christian Workers, Pax-Romans (a Roman Catholic organization for intellectual and cultural affairs), the Commission of the Churches on International Affairs, the Catholic International Union for Social Service, and the Friends' World Committee are a few of a long list.

4. *Social Purpose*: Almost as numerous as the international organizations with an economic orientation are those whose purposes may be classified generally is social betterment. Their purposes range from the suppression of the slave rats to the fostering of temperance, including the improvement of social rift welfare activities and the improvement of health and sanitation. Representative organizations are the International Committee of the Red Cross, the International Conference of Social Work, the International Council of Women, the International Society for the Welfare of Cripples, and those two familiar ones, the World's Alliance of Young Men's Christian Associations and the Young Women's Christian Association.

5. *Technical and Scholarly*: Technical and specialized organizations exist in most of the fields of advanced learning. The International Statistical Institute, the International Society of Criminology, the International Political Science. Association, the International Law Association, and many other similar organizations exist.

In all of them the purpose is the exchange of information and experiences upon an organized basis for the improvement of the technical competence of all concerned.

There remain still many other private international organizations that do not fit into any of these five categories, but the listing does at least suggest something of the scope of human activity that is affected by these bodies.

Consultation with the United Nations. Following a practice originally formalized by the League of Nations, Article 71 of the Charter of the United Nations provides for establishment of consultative relationships between private (non-governmental) organizations and the Economic and Social Council for the purposes of mutually considering problems of common interest. The Council has prepared and keeps on file a register of such organizations, which maintain a consultative relationship.

They are divided into three categories: category 'A' includes 'organizations which are closely linked with the economic or social life of the areas which they represent'; a third category includes organisations that maintain less formal relations with the Council but are available upon an ad hoc basis for consolation when such action is indicated.

By the beginning of 1954, there were nine organizations in category 'A' 92 in category 'B' and 115 international groups were on the register for ad hoc consultations. The following nine organizations formed category 'A':

International Chamber of Commerce

International Confederation of Free Trade Unions

International Co-operative Alliance

International Federation of Agricultural Producers

International Federation of Christian Trade Unions

International Organization of Employers

Inter-Parliamentary Union

World Federation of Trade Unions

World Federation of United Nations Associations.

Public International Unions

There are international organizations whose orientation and purposes are clearly toward the individual and the ends be purses. Just as in the case of the private organizations discussed above. They can be distinguished from the latter since they have as members not individuals but sovereign states. Since they are governmental, they operate upon a more formal basis than do the private groups and as a result both gain and lose in effectiveness. Their internal organisation, their membership, and their functions very so greatly that beyond certain general statements it is impossible to classify them in any meaningful fashion. All have some kind of central bureau with permanent administrators, and provision is always made for periodic conferences; beyond that, each one organizes itself largely in terms of the international instrument (a treaty or convention).

The public international organizations of specialized purposes can be divided into two groups. The first consists of those more important ones with 'wide international responsibilities' which have been brought into relationship with the United Nations and are known as the specialized agencies.' The second includes all the remainder—several hundreds of varying size and degree of formalization—which are either geographically or functionally so specialized as lent to merit relationship with the United Nations.

Independent Public International Unions

1. Transportation and Communication, and Economic: Since the organization and structure of these bodies differ so widely, the only possible way to summarize their operations is in terms of the functions to which they address themselves. Among the many independent public international organizations that exist, the following types can be found.

(1) The first group is formed by those that concern themselves with problems of transportation and communication. Among them are such international reparian and administrative bodies as the European Danube Commission, railway bodies such as the International Union of Railway Freight Transportation, and various regional bodies that deal with telecommunications.

(2) A second classification is that of organizations that have as their primary purpose the improvement of some aspect(s) of economic life.

Perhaps the most impressive example of how far states will go in creating cards to deal with economic matters is furnished by the European Coal and Steel Community, the formal institution executing the Schuman Plan for the pooling of the coal and steel industry of the six western European sues of France, West Germany, Italy, Belgium, Luxembourg, and the Netherlands. This group has transcended the traditional basis of national sovereignty has created as new instrument of government.

1. Social, Cultural, and Scientific. Many international unions deal with social questions similar to those dealt with by the private organizations considered in the preceding section. Although many of these unions have been absorbed by various of the commissions and specialized agencies of the United Nations, a number of them still retain their autonomy and operate with reduced scope in limited areas.

Other international unions deal with cultural and scientific purposes. Such basic data as weights and measures and a standard map of the world are in the care of the International Bureau of Weights and Measures and the Central Bureau of the International Map of the World. The International Hydrographic Bureau coordinates and makes available to everyone the work of the various national states in the areas of hydrograph and navigation.

United Nations Agencies

The United Nations system includes two types of organizations that deal with questions within the particular interest of the international community: first, the commission, committees, and special bodies that are an integral part of the United Nations itself; second, the `specialized agencies' that exist as independent international organizations but are `in relationship' with the parent body.

Commissions and other United Nations Agencies: The membership of the first type of agency consists of members of the United Nations appointed to the respective bodies by action of the General

Assembly. Most of these bodies have names and functions that are self-explanatory.

The first type is the functional commission. These are created to deal with a particular subject, presumably of general interest to all members. A listing of the objects with which these commissions deal illustrate the scope of United Nations activity in economic and social affairs. Commissions only on the following topics: economics and employment, transportation and status of women, narcotic drugs, fiscal questions, and population question. Each of these bodies deals with its problem by making recommendations the Economic and Social Council and to the General Assembly.

A second type, economic in scope and geographic in scope and geographic in organization, is the regional commission. Three of these exist at present: the Economic Commission for Europe (ECE), the Economic Commission for Asia and the Far East (ECAFE), and the Economic Commission for Latin America (ECLA) Membership is drawn from the states in each region and other nations with particular interest. Their action is principally co-ordinating and expending.

Procedural matters are the principal concern of standing committees. Two typical examples are the committee on Negotiations with Inter-Governmental Agencies (public international unions) and the Committee for Causation with Non-Governmental Organizations (private international organizations).

Less important are the too remaining types, the ad hoc committees and the special bodies. The first group are temporary bodies to deal with the recurrent problems for limited times; examples include the Commission on Genocide and the United Nations Appeal for Children.

The second type consists of semi-permanent administrative agencies that exercise supervisory of coordinating functions over particular problems.

Two of the best known of these are the Permanent Central Opium Board, which supervises the International Narcotics Trade, and the United Nations International Children Emergency Fund (UNICEF).

The Specialized Agencies: The specialized agencies of the United

Nations are different international organizations, each created by a multilateral international agreement. Each maintains its own membership, its own bodies and administrative staff, and its own area of operations.

As a result of a special agreement between each of them and the United Nations, a chew working relationship involving co-ordination, consultation, and mutual assistance exists between the parent organization and all the spectacled agencies and between the specialized agencies themselves.

In the following summary listing data relative to headquarters, functions, budget, and membership are as of the end of 1954.

1. The International Labour Organization (ILO) was established in 1919 and came into relationship with the United Nations in 1946. Seventy-nine state constitute the membership headquarters are maintained in Switzerland, with branch offices throughout the world.
2. The Food and Agriculture Organization (FAO) of the United Nations actually came into being in 1954 and was brought into relationship with the United Nations the following year. Seventy-one states formed the membership in 1954; headquarters being maintained at Rome.
3. The United Nations Educational, Scientific, and Cultural Organization (UNESCO) was created late in 1946 and entered into its United Nations relationship several weeks later in the same year.
4. The International Civil Aviation Organization (ICAO) was created in 1947 and almost immediately entered into a relationship with the United Nations. Sixty-three states (at that time) maintain memberships headquarters of the organization being at Montreal.
5. The International Bank for Reconstruction and Development came into being late in 1945 and entered into relationship with the United Nations two years later. Headquarters are located in Washington, with a European office in Paris.
6. The International Monetary Fund (IMF) has the same

dates of cooption and of adherence to the United Nations as does the Bank, its organization. Its headquarters are in Washington in the same building that houses the Bank.

7. The World Health Organization (WHO), officially went into operation in 1947 and almost immediately established its relationship with the United Nations. Headquarters are in Geneva and nine regional offices are maintained.
8. The Original Postal Union (UPU) was created in 1874; in 1948 its constitution was amended to incorporate an agreement bringing it into relationship with the United Nations. The UPU is the closest approximation to a truly universal international organization. Its headquarters are in Berne, Switzerland.
9. The International Refugee Organization (IRO) was created officially in 1948 and came into relationship with the United Nations at the same time; it terminated its operations and ended its existence in January 1952.
10. The International Telecommunications Union (ITU) grew out of coder international agreements upon telegraphy and radiotelegraphy prior a World War II. The ITU was actually created in 1934 but was reorganized at trims of a new convention in 1947.

    The new ITU formally entered into existence in 1949 and the agreement with the United Nations came into force at the same time. Ninety countries and territories have joined; headquarters are in Geneva.
11. The World Meteorological Organization (WMO) grew out of the International Meteorological Organization that was founded in 1878. The WMO was formally established in 1951. The membership is made up of 58 states and 24 territories, a total of 82. Headquarters are in Geneva; regional offices are maintained in six areas of the world.

What do all these institutions, organizations, and agencies mean with the guard to the status of the international community? They represent a right accumulation of organized effort by individuals, groups, and governments upon the common social and economic problems of men.

The majority of the state of the world have demonstrated the insistence of their peoples that concrete action be taken in the direction of solving some of the continuing problems of individual life in a world grown more complex and insecure.

The international community is not any longer the mere dream of amiable but impractical philosophers; it has grown to the level where it is a force powerful enough to bring about broad and binding action by governments.

THE INTERNATIONAL COMMUNITY AND WORLD POLITICS

State and Community Struggle

the implications for world politics of the existence of the international community and its progressive realization, we must first recognize the constant conflict that is inherent in the relations of the nation-state with the international community.

To the extent that an individual adheres to the international community his nationalist identification is weakened. It is because this dichotomy is so clear in contemporary world affairs that the advance and the development of the international community is fought so bitterly by chauvinists in every state.

There are some governments in the world whose national interest leads them to foster the growth of international institutions of a community nature, but they are and promise to be for a long time in the minority.

Advantages of the State: In the struggle for individual loyalty that is going on between the state and the international community, it is self-evident that the state enjoys certain advantages. There are a least three reasons which help explain this situation.

In the first place, the state is universal in its appeal and comes before individuals at every turn in their lives. The international community, on the other hand, presents itself to most people only in terms of a single interest or a small group of them. Merely in terms of the number of appeals aimed at individuals, the state makes contact with its citizens many more times and upon many more issues than does the community. A case can, of course, be made for the universality of the international community, but the great majority of men, if they are aware of the community at all, think of it in terms only of the one or two ways in witch it impinges upon them directly. A second appeal of the state is emotional. The state earns much of the family of its citizens by using the symbols of nationalism and the formulas of biology as tolls.

For most individuals the international community is defected upon rational grounds involving a logical and dispassionate judgment of the relative merits of the two systems. In a conflict for loyalty by seen emotional and rational appeals, the former enjoys most of the advantages. There are individuals whose attachment to the concept of the community is as emotional as is the sense of nationalist dedication of most other people, but thus far they constitute only a relative handful.

So long as governments can evoke mass emotional reactions to the manipulation of nationalist stimuli, the rate of growth of the international community will continue to be slow.

In the third place, the state can command the obedience of its citizens in a way at present barred to the community: the reliance upon coercion. The state may compel agreement, or at least the absence of open dissent; the only adherents the community has are those who become so through voluntary action. Governments in many states have undertaken deliberate policies with the object of obstructing the growth of community institutions upon as international level and to destroying the sense of international community.

Reasons for the Growth of the Community Sense

Why has the community sense continued to attract more supporters at the very same time that the intensity of international conflict has increased?

We have seen that increasing individual contact has broadened the comprehension of the outside world by individuals, and that co-operative action has been forced from states as a result.

Perhaps, the greatest single factor in the growth of the international-community sense however has been the widespread revulsion of individuals against the perpetuation of a system that has brought two catastrophic wars in a generation and constantly threatens to produce a third. From millions of men comes a plea for some new approach to international life, one that will free them from the awful uncertainty and insecurity that are the lot of everyone today.

Men have placed themselves at the service of their states for generations; now, with the technology of mass destruction having become an exact science (or, as some students view it, a fine art), many of them are becoming unwilling to go on. In this attitude there is no element of either cowardice or disloyalty; the way of competition, crisis, and conflict, they seem to say, has brought only ruin and stalemate. Mankind is instead of seeking positive attack upon international problems incorporating agreement and good faith.

4

International Political Problems

Political problems are the core issues of International politics. By the 'political' problem area we mean particularly those crisis points in today's world which bear directly upon the institution of the nation-state, its present and future prospects, and the relations of states in their corporate capacities to each other.

These constitute some of the more 'traditional' and familiar aspects of international politics, which are based upon the legal personality of the state. In this area is found the greatest popular awareness of international relations; the political contacts of states grip the imaginations of men in more compelling fashion than does any other level of relations.

The Bipolar World: An Historical Account

Though now obsolete, here we are giving an historical account of Bipolar world. The most dramatic and compelling single feature of world politics since the end of World War II has been the existence of the 'bipolar' world. Every aspect of world relations has been affected and often dominated by the fact that the two giants, the United States and the Soviet Union (now defund), have assumed positions of mutual hostility in general policy and upon almost every specific issue as it has arisen.

Nor have they been content to conduct their cold war with one another in isolation; they have insisted upon attempting to enlist all of the other states of the world under one banner or the other and upon investing any question of international relations with a peculiar relevance derived from its being involved in the Russo-American conflict.

It would have been too much to expect all the smaller states of the world to accept this situation with equanimity and good cheer. The less powerful members of the world community have often felt that the bipolar world has left them too little room in which to seek the advancement of their own interests and has presented them too bluntly and too often with the prospect of a total war in the stakes of which they have had only a minor interest.

Consequently, there have been numerous counter-forces at work, seeking to reduce the grip of the great powers and to break up the overly narrow bipolar world.

Of late this tendency has grown stronger and more apparent. If the bipolar world is indeed disintegrating, the consequent realignments are bound to be accompanied by a whole series of new stresses and strains, as severe (although of a different sort) as those produced since 1945 by the cold war.

The Causes of Bipolarity

Perhaps at no time since the Muslim menaced the Christian world in the fifteenth century has so much of the future of mankind been bound up in the relations of any two power blocs.

The bipolar world is so important a factor in the lives of all of us today that we should make every effort to understand how and why the world arrived at such a state. The causes of bipolarity must be comprehended before any decision can be arrived at for coping with it.

Concentration of Power: The most important single cause of the bifurcated nature of contemporary world affairs is the reshuffling of the power pattern of the world which grew out of world War II.

Although the processes of national decline and advance originated long before that conflict (indeed, we know already that they are continuous), they reached a climax and in some cases completion during and after the war.

At the end of the fighting all but the most biased observers were aware that the end of an era had arrived. Some of the great powers of the first part of the century had disappeared entirely, others had been drastically weakened, while still others had gone into a temporary eclipse.

Certain new ones, formerly only minor participants in world affairs, were occupying or were moving toward the centre of the stage. Italy and France represented the former great powers reduced to secondary status; Britain's hurts were serious; Germany and Japan were temporarily important; meanwhile, the United States and the Soviet Union dominated world affairs by virtue of superior power. India and China, the future giants, were as yet unable to mobilize their great potential.

In the postwar world only the United States and the USSR have been able to exercise any meaningful freedom of choice in determining their foreign policies.

Had events worked out so as to permit them to co-operate actively, the course of world affairs since 1945 would have been very different. Conflict and competition have been the nature of their relationship, however, and everyone everywhere has felt the impact of the clash.

The first factor tending toward the present bipolarity is, therefore, that only two mutually hostile states have been able to carry on foreign affairs with any real freedom since the war.

Ideological Policy. We must now look in more detail at these two antagonists in order to see how their power relationships have led to the present bipolar stalemate. Both the United States and the Soviet Union are, in comparison with most of the other participants in world affairs, relatively young and inexperienced.

This youth and lack of background are most apparent in the relative inability of both governments to understand the limits upon and the responsibility accompanying great political power.

Thrust suddenly into positions of world leadership without sufficient maturity to provide a basis for action, both have been so far unable to rationalize fully the often conflicting demands of time and place.

Both governments have given indications of an uncertainty regarding the demands of true national interest as well as much hesitancy and reluctance to seize upon the most expedient means of advancing that interest.

Without the poise and confidence obtainable only from years

of dealing with the slippery and elusive realities of world politics, the leaders of both states have been obliged to fall back upon the promptings of ideologies and the stimuli of mass emotions as a guide to conduct.

The leadership of the Soviet is beyond doubt guilty of taking the first great steps in this direction and of precipitating mass ideological struggle in the postwar world. American reaction to Soviet ideological assault, although somewhat delayed in its appearance, ultimately developed as much force as had the Russian attack.

Thus Russo-American have proceeded in recent years upon a primarily ideological and emotional basis. This arose in the first instance out of a lack of ability to devise a realistic course of action and has kept going ever since largely on its own momentum.

At various points in earlier chapters we have delineated some of the characteristics of an ideologically oriented policy. It is sufficient at this point only to remind ourselves that an ideological battle in international politics is marked by two principal characteristics: the constant expansion of policy by both parties, and the extreme difficulty of compromise.

Both arise from the fact that ideologies are viewed by their adherents as summaries of absolute moral truth.

The cold war has demonstrated these symptoms. Neither the USSR nor the United States has been willing either to compromise its ideological faith or to accept a definitive limitation upon its objectives.

The Elimination of Power Vacuums. Thus we come to the third in the sequence of causes of the bipolar world. The two great powers have confronted each other with a fixed policy but each has proved to be unable to make any major impression upon the other by its own efforts.

As a result each has sought to gain allies for itself and to deny them to its adversary in the hope of gaining a decisive advantage.

The outcome of this race for support has been the attempted elimination of 'power vacuums' all over the world: those areas into which the power of one or the other of the great states has not yet flowed.

These power vacuums were of two types: states in which the domestic government was so weak and unstable as to make it impossible for any clear foreign-policy commitments to be made, or else states in which strong government existed but where a policy decision had been taken in favour of neutrality in the great-power conflict. Iran is an example of the first type, India of the second.

To both great powers it is unthinkable that a power vacuum should exist anywhere in the world while a titanic struggle is going on whose prize is the victory of good over evil. Both have sought unceasingly to eliminate all such areas, each using all possible combinations of persuasion, pressure, and open coercion to advance its case.

A dual motive has always been present in the struggle for control of any power vacuum: the desire to gain an ally is mixed with the need to deny one to the enemy. In any case, by the early part of 1950 it appeared as if the bipolarity of the world was complete.

All the power vacuum either had been obliterated or seemed well on their way to extinction and the world appeared finally to be divided between the two armed camps.

Bipolarity in Practice

The Loss of Flexibility: In practice bipolarity left international politics in a curiously truncated state. In the first place, all freedom of manoeuvre was lost. The bulk of the states of the world were tied tightly to the leader of the group they had joined (or into which they had been forced). The two giants had likewise surrendered their freedom.

Each had pressed its policy to the outermost possible limits, to the point where it met the expanding policy of the other.

Neither could any longer make a move without provoking an immediate retaliation by the other; in practice, therefore, each confined itself to countering any threats raised by the other.

Nor was any greater freedom possible in the relations of the major states with their minor allies. The only reason for the existence of the great blocs was great-power hostility and all intra-group moves were for the single purpose of making the alliances tighter and more unified in purpose and organization.

The Inexpediency of Force. The bipolar world was one in which the resolution of differences by means of the classic mechanisms of diplomacy and compromise was no longer possible. What was peculiarly frustrating to statesmen was that the other historic device for solving international problems—force—was equally futile.

The use of violence on any basis short of total war was virtually impossible since neither bloc was willing to submit to mere demonstrations or threats.

Total war was, in its turn, such a frightful prospect and the outcome so uncertain the neither party seriously considered it as a means of resolving any of the major issues.

Neither side possessed a sufficiently great advantage over the other to hold out the prospect of the relatively quick victory that alone would make the effort worth while; the only certain outcome of great-power total war was widespread devastation and staggering casualties among participants and neutrals alike.

With freedom of manoeuvre gone and in view of the extreme unfeasibility of a settlement by force, the bipolar world presented a picture of unrelieved rigidity and stalemate. Mutual frustration and bafflement have been the lot of both groups. Bickering and disagreement were the normal atmosphere of such contacts as the two cap$ have had with each other; crisis situations—such as the Berlin blockade—did not reach clean and total resolution but were temporized upon almost any basis that would serve to minimize tension.

The only open military struggle between the groups, the Korean war and the Indo-China war, were no more able to produce any clear-cut decision. Disputes dragged in interminably simply because no viable basis for compromise could be found in a bipolar situation and any absolute answer was equally impossible to discover. The movement and change that we have seen to be inherent and integral aspects of 'normal world politics were largely destroyed by the operation of the principle of bipolarity.

In this way the contemporary political scene has to a large

degree not corresponded with the general picture of international relations presented in earlier chapters.

The Breakup of the Bipolar World

The imposition of the bipolar structure upon the world was a result of the shifting patterns of power relationship in the world after 1945. We have seen that the factors of power resist being frozen into a static mold; the bipolar world was from the beginning subject to pressures tending toward its eventual breakup. Most important of these is the absolute and relative superiority in power enjoyed by the two major states toward the rest of the world has been steadily diminishing from its postwar high.

Other power centres have sprung up and other problems than the exclusive one of Russo-American relations have demanded and are receiving attention from peoples and governments.

Neither great state is able to dominate and control the members of its own alliance with the same degree of confidence as formerly; consequently, intra-group relations have become a matter of new and great urgency for both the USSR and the United States.

New power blocs are in the process of formation and are making inroads upon the membership of the old ones. Power-wise, it is becoming much more difficult to keep the world locked up in bipolar cage.

Causes of the Decline of Bipolarity: Some of the immediate reasons for the decline of bipolarity and the breakup of the two-power world ought to be briefly indicated. Perhaps the most convincing, from the point of view of the smaller states, is the intolerability of perpetual stalemate. The domestic and international problems of the lesser powers have continued to evolve and have reached the point where serious attempts at their solution must be made.

The issues of hunger, disease, economic and cultural underdevelopment, and national self-expression will no longer remain in the background while the only concern of statesmen everywhere continues to be the relationship of two global powers.

Since the Russo-American problem continues unsolved and threatens to remain so indefinitely, from every quarter of the globe have some demands that governments take direct and productive action to deal with issues that have been left unconsidered. Stalemate may be undesirable as far as the bipolar powers themselves are concerned, but they have proved to be unable to discover a formula for its dissolution.

The smaller powers of Asia, of Europe, of Africa, and of the western Hemisphere have begun to make clear that for their part they are unwilling to submit permanently to the rigidity of a bipolar world that produces no solutions but only multiplies tensions.

As per this point of view the great powers may, if they wish, to continue to keep their policies locked in a hopeless and endless struggle; however, they can no longer put off the rest of the world on the same basis. The smaller states aver that they are seeking some other destiny than perpetual tension forever unresolved. Another factor entering the picture at this point is the decreasing danger of war. During the early days of the cold war, while the lines of alliance were forming and hardening, there was a real and justified fear of war and its attendant human and material damage. The smaller states were much disturbed lest the inexperience and militant ideology of each major government unleash the catastrophe that many of them had so much historic reason to dread.

This was only one of the factors that led these states to join one or another alliance, but there is no doubt that it played a major part in the thinking of many, notably the states of western Europe.

In any case, for most of the participants other than the leaders, the desire to avoid war if possible and to be in a strong position if war should come was a great factor in the creation of the rigid blocs that characterize the bipolar world.

Today, however, much of the earlier fear of war has receded. Rightly or wrongly, the leaders of many states both camps are unconvinced that the disaster of total war is imminent or even probable. In that case the alliance of which they form a part is no longer a protection but an encumbrance. The loss of the right of independent action and the indefinite postponement of their own national objectives have become too great a price to pay for protection against a danger that grows steadily more remote.

Evidence often shows that the Soviet Union is finding its allies similarly intractably, particularly the government of China and some of the minor states in Eastern Europe. Czechoslovakia and East Germany both indicated by open popular resistance during early 1953 that oppression by Russia was more of a real problem to them that any threat from the West; China likewise followed an independent course at the Geneva Conference in 1954. It is unnecessary to evaluate the validity of the position of these states as regards the lessened danger of war; it is sufficient to point out that the attitude exists and that it is having a perceptible influence on the development of bipolar politics.

Another aspect of the same frame of mind is a spread belief in the possibility of neutrality, either in the cold war or in all-out one. Several years ago, while the great powers possessed ample ability to enforce their will upon their lesser allies, it seemed to many people as if the American and Russian governments were less hostile toward each other than both were toward any state that sought to stay aloof from the conflict.

This period has passed. The shifting distribution of power has given many states the ability to conduct policies of independent action, equally free of dictation from both camps, that would have been unthinkable a few years ago.

India's stubborn refusal to become embroiled in the cold war was the first step toward the appearance of real neutralism its example has been followed by several others. As a result, the thinking of many statesmen today is drastically different from what it was at the height of bipolarity.

They recognize the extent to which the great powers are committed in their struggle against each other. The United States and the USSR are no longer able to apply coercive pressure upon their allies to the same degree.

Policy makers in some smaller states also are speculating upon the possibility of avoiding involvement in any total war that might develop out of the Russo-American controversy and are tending to arrange their policies in this direction.

It cannot be ignored, however, that in seeking neutrality the governments of the small states are responding to a deep-rooted and broadly based popular demand, and that the operation of the political process in recent years has given them reason to hope for success.

We have already referred to the most pervasive symptoms of the dissolution of the bipolar world: the increasing independence of policy and action on the part of smaller states in all parts of the world. India set the pattern; other Asiatic states such as Indonesia and Burma have followed suit. In the Middle East, Iran and Egypt have for the most part severed their connections with the Western bloc and are seeking to pilot a course that is independently determined, though far from pro-communist.

In the Soviet world, Yugoslavia's break with Kremlin in 1948 came about primarily because of Marshal Tito's refusal to govern all his actions by the dictates of Moscow.

Following the death of Stalin in March 1953, signs multiple that the USSR was finding China ever more determined to follow a policy formed in terms of Chinese interests rather than Russian.

Two spectacular breaks in the two alliances occurred during June 1953. In Korea, at the very moment when a truce seemed imminent, Dr. Rhee, the president of the Republic of Korea, took independent action in freeing the non-communist prisoners of war, whose fate had been the object of many weary month of negotiation; although this action threatened to upset prospects for peace the United States was forced to acquiesce and ultimately appeased Rhee with a favourable agreement. During the same month, rebellion against domestic communist and Russian domination flared in East Germany, forcing the Soviet to declare martial law and to employ naked violence to suppress the revolt. Although Soviet control was restored, major concessions to the Germans were necessary before peace returned. The uprising destroyed the illusion of solidarity among the 'people's republics' behind the Iron Curtain much as South Korea's rebellion showed up the cracks in the structure of the Western world.

The world community no longer consists only of two armed camps confronting each other; it also includes a number of states not part of the two groups which are attempting—with uneven success—to insulate themselves from the more pernicious effects of bipolarity.

A visible symptoms of the breakup of the bipolar world is the change in the outlook of the people of many states. No longer do they view world affairs only through eyes directed by the command of the great powers; instead, they are once again reverting to the familiar diversity so typical of world politics when it is carried on upon a more traditional basis.

These newer attitudes may be considered as retrogressions, one cannot but regret the revival of parochial nationalism in states such as France and West Germany, where once it had been thought to be extinct. In like manner the newly freed states of Asia have demonstrated their independence by a reckless employment of the same nationalistic techniques. In other states, the gradual decline in the paralyzing numbness of bipolarity has released more forward-looking forces in many people.

For effectiveness bipolarity requires a bipolar mental attitude; when people cease to think of world politics as involving nothing but the choice between the Soviet Union and the United States, the psychological base of the bipolar structure is undermined.

Effects of Breakup

If the bipolar world is indeed in the process of dissolution, the next few years are destined to be a period of drastic reorganization and readjustment. The calculation appropriate to a two-power world will have to be either scrapped or drastically revised. Diplomacy will again play its historic part as a harmonizing and adjusting procedure. This transformation from a rigid and narrow frame for world politics to a fluid and flexible one will not be easy. The great powers—and many of the smaller ones as well—have made so many firm policy commitments based upon the perpetuation of bipolarity that to change them will produce stresses and uprisings of major proportions.

This era of change is likely to prove particularly testing for Americans. When the dreams of peace and security faded in the postwar period and Americans were brought up against the stern realities of great-power conflict, and passed through a period of emotional stress and finally succeeded in adjusting themselves to a world which they felt to be fundamentally hostile.

Russian-American controversy is a phenomenon which, if not

pleasant, has at least the virtue of familiarity; for us to be deprived of it by the operations of a multi-power political process would leave many of us almost defenseless psychologically.

Americans, grown increasingly cynical as their many sincere offers for peace and co-operation have been rebuffed, today display a marked emotional tendency to shrink from the prospect of a resolution of the cold war.

Public opinion therefore discounts in advance any new hope for improvement in the cold war. Russian 'peace' feelers are immediately rejected by press and public alike, thus handicapping American diplomats who must explore them. No matter how great the strain, Americans must prepare themselves for a new era in which Russian-American conflict will not be the only significant political relationship in the world.

The New Power Blocs: One effect of the breakup of bipolarity is the further development of new power centres. The process is already advanced to the point where there is little likelihood that it will be arrested. The most important single power group that is today relatively free from dictation by either great power is of course India and its associates in the Arab-Asian bloc.

As the reference is made to the manner in which India has mobilized some of the states of south and southeast Asia to form a powerful group in the United Nations and in the Asiatic region as well. A significant tribute to India's strategic role was the fact that Indian forces were employed to police the prisoner exchange that followed the Korean truce of July 1953. At that time India was the world's outstanding neutral. But other areas also are growing in power significance. In the Middle East the Arab states, although beset by nationalist and dynastic rivalries, are struggling to discover a formula for joint action that will liberate them forever from 'Western imperialism' and yet preserve them from Soviet expansionism.

In Europe, the movement for European consolidation has been moving forward at a jerky but fairly rapid pace. True, it has been under the active sponsorship of the United States and is often viewed as part of American cold-war strategy; nevertheless there is little doubt in the minds of many Europeans that they are preparing for the day when a truly independent Europe will become free of control by either Moscow or Washington which is nearly achieved now.

It is also obvious that the government of the Union of South Africa is also seeking immunization from the cold war by establishing itself as an independent power centre.

Now, the case of China must be considered. Whether it is to be communist or democratic, one thing about the future of China is certain: it is going some day to attain great-power status and it will, in the long run, be nobody's satellite. No matter how one may view the present status and role of China, its future is clearly that of an independent power centre.

Another possible outgrowth of the end of bipolarity is an increasing attempt on the part of the independent power centres to mediate the cold war. This has also already become apparent; India's neutral position in the United Nations has enabled it to move positively upon several occasions in the direction of an intervention between the disputing powers. Its most active policy in this regard was its persistent search for a formula of settlement of the prisoner-of-war issue in Korea. Britain and France, although they have not yet gone to the extreme of intervening actively and directly between the United States and Soviet bloc, have nevertheless restrained American action when they feared it might go too far.

Many times since the end of the fighting in Korea Winston Churchill urged a renewal of top-level conversations between the USSR the United Kingdom, and the United States in the hopes of bringing about a major relaxation of tension. This became a reality in the negotiation over the Austrian Peace Treaty in May 1955.

Since all the new and growing power centres of the world are marked by a real or incipient impatience toward both great powers for (as they see it) constantly threatening the world with war, it is only natural to expect them to redouble their efforts at pacification as their capacity to exert significant power continues to increase.

As long as one of the overriding concerns of the new power centres continues to be peace, they will continue their attempts not only to prevent hot war from growing out of cold but also to bring about a material improvement in the climate of world affairs by resorting Russo-American relations to the level of at least mutual tolerance and co-existence.

As the bipolar world its definite character and new power blocs appear to rival the formerly dominant states a real possibility exists that one outcome will be the strengthening of the United Nations. The greatest obstacle to the success of the world organization has been Soviet-American conflict; it is also clear that most of the other states of the world have real hopes that the United Nations has a better prospect of success in store for it if the grip of bipolarity could be loosed.

None of the other potential great powers has any inherent vested interest in aggrandizement; all need peace and co-operation in order to fully realize their potential, and most of them recognize this fact. If the two great states should lose their capacity jointly to control the United Nations machinery and instead be obliged to share the directing power with other peace-minded states, the opportunity for a real expansion in the world role of the organization would be at hand.

This expansion of the scope of the United Nations would take place throughout the organization but most definitely in two particular areas. In the first place, the peace-enforcing activities of the Security Council would be far more effective.

If the USSR could be brought to understand that its real national interest can best be served by co-operative action within the organization instead of a reckless disregard for it, the veto would cease to be a serious consideration.

If both the great powers should become persuaded that the future of mankind is of more importance than the outcome of any particular power controversy and that both would prosper most in a peaceful world, they would be more willing to cooperate in the enforcement of peace.

The Security Council would then become what it was originally intended to be: the collective voice of the world insisting that all international conflicts be settled peacefully. The other great expansion of United Nations activity would be in the area of economic and social activity. Permanent peace is possible only when the social, economic, and psychological factors that cause war are eliminated. Nothing is more absolutely a step in the right direction than the United Nations programme in this area.

Probable Dangers

It may be noted that the foregoing is an over-optimistic picture of the future. This may well be a just criticism. The period of readjustment necessitated by the dissolution of bipolarity will be accompanied by much indecision and wavering on the part of all states as they seek a viable policy in a new situation.

Periods of readjustment are always full of tension and potential danger as new and unexpected situations demand action. Statesmen, operating without any clearly defined lines of policy, might be tempted to take drastic or thoughtless action that would never even be considered under a more settled system. In a complex and changing set of relationships the outcome of any crisis is more uncertain than when the pattern of politics is more stable. No one can be certain that the world will pass safely through the transition period that will follow the final breakup of the bipolar world. If it does not, if war and crisis eventuate before the final re-establishment of peace, it may will turn out that the bipolar structure of the world was the only means open to men to preserve the peace.

Political Organization: New Bases

One more problem area of great importance to contemporary man is the search for a new basis of political organization. Governments and private individuals in all parts of the world are becoming dissatisfied with the presently constituted nation-state as the primary political unit. Many of them are seeking to discover some new and different method of organizing political power and of achieving their political purposes more effectively. Almost all possible avenues are being considered, and many of them have been explored to some extent by particular governments. The overall impact upon world politics of this concern with the future of the nation-state cannot help but be great; it promises to become more and more significant with the passage of time.

Perhaps it would be premature to speak of the 'end of the nation-state as being imminent. It is undeniable, however, that policy makers in most governments today are seriously handicapped by the limitations of the state form of organization and are searching for some new basis upon which to organize. We have stressed in the first part of this chapter that since 1945 only the United States and the Soviet Union have possessed sufficient power to carry on a relatively self-determined foreign policy.

What were the factors that inhibited all other states and made them succumb to the pressures of bipolarity? What is wrong with the nation-state today?

As in so many cases dealing with world politics, the answer to the question must be phrased first in terms of power. The two giants of world affairs today represent the greatest concentrations of political and military power, actual and potential, that have existed since the modern state system was born.

Never before in modern times has so much of the effective force of state authority been concentrated in so few hands. No citizen or official of one of the smaller states of the world can contemplate this disparity without becoming disturbed. To face the future calmly in a condition of being domed to permanent inferiority has already proved to be impossible for many minor states and is becoming more difficult for all of them. The old type of national state, with an area of less than half a million square mile sand a population ranging from five to seventy million, is nearly obsolete compared to continental giants such as the USSR and the USA.

The political technology of the modern day has made it possible to mobilize the potential power of millions of square miles and hundreds of millions of people under a single government, and anything less cannot ever rival the massive leaders of today.

The instruments of modern power are mass-produced and mass-employed, and sheer lack of size has made the old states of Europe and the newer small states of Asia and the rest of the world unable to compete upon any basis of equality. The problems of the technology of the mass are insoluble for the small state. If this were all, it would be serious enough for the great majority of men who live in the smaller states of the world.

The old (pre-1939) type of 'great power' is not only incapable today of very much freedom in its policy, but it is unsure of even being able to guarantee its continued existence. France, for example, knows that its independence could be snuffed out in an instant by either great power; so do all the little states of the Middle East and Southeast Asia.

If independence today is such an illusory thing, dependent upon the whim of the major powers, it is no wonder that so many people are willing to exchange sovereignty for some new organizational form that promises more real security.

In another way the state form of organization fails today in most parts of the world to measure up to the demands placed upon it. In many important areas the problems that governments are called upon to deal with transcend national boundaries in their scope they demand action broader than any state could take unilaterally. Included in this category are the pressing social, psychological, and economic tensions that are so apparent in every part of the world. The devastation of World War II created problems of economic reconstruction and recovery in Europe that far exceeded the capacity of any single state to handle; the development of industrialization and the elevation of the standard of living of the people are tasks beyond the ability of any of the states of Asia or Africa.

These are only a few of the problems which men insist that governments solve. Because of the limited physical and human base upon which most nation-states are organized, they are helpless to take meaningful steps toward the relief of these pressures. Even in the political field, the problems presented by the postwar world overlap state boundaries, and governments are at a loss how to proceed. The political technique of subversion and the policy problem of devising means to cope with Soviet-sponsored and Soviet-directed Communist parties have demonstrated again the inability of the nation-state to deal with global political and security questions.

Political Organization: New Forms

The need for new forms of political organization that will offset the most serious shortcomings of the state form has taken several directions. In every case something more fundamental is being sought than the traditional association of states in which each participant guards its sovereignty jealously and procedure is based solely upon consultation and prior agreement.

International Organization: The first new structure that should be mentioned in this connection is general international organization on the lines of the United Nations.

The organization is all-inclusive in its membership, is permanent, and enjoys a broad range of action. We have already seen how the United Nations has jurisdiction in the political sphere through the operation of the Security Council and, in certain cases, the General Assembly; indeed, the very existence of the Security Council offers proof of the fact that many statesmen feel that individual states can no longer be permitted to handle their disputes themselves. In addition, the United Nations is designed to provide organization for solving the non-political question that are global or at least supra-national in their effect.

The Economic and Social Council, the Trusteeship Council, the commissions, and the specialized agencies all have as their reason for existence the need for coordinated solutions to problems common to individuals in many states. General international organization is the most ambitious step yet taken by states in the direction of a new basis for political organization.

The states of the world are not prepared to make workable an organization in which membership is universal and with a projected scope of authority far beyond what any international body has yet enjoyed. There are still too many political conflicts among the major states, and too much of a tendency to attempt unilateral action, for the peace-enforcing machinery to be effective. There are also too many technical questions unsolved and too much intrusion of political considerations for the economic and social work to be truly significant.

And yet, the nations of the world seem to agree that the United Nations is necessary and must be preserved. Even the divisive pressures of bipolarity proved incapable of destroying it, and the process of learning its capabilities and its limitations goes on constantly.

Concept of World Government: We have seen that the basic motivation of the world government movement has been its conviction that the nation-state system cannot, by its very nature, preserve the peace. Factors of both technology and human psychology figure largely in this process of reasoning. The destructiveness of war and the explosive potentialities of the state system are stressed as reasons why men must transfer their primary loyalty from the state to some more broadly based body.

The all-at-once creation of a world government by the deliberate act of will of the states of the world is such a remote possibility at th(present level of world understanding as not to deserve serious consideration.

The very extent of the movement, however, and the quality of the leadership it has attracted are proof that the need for some such action is urgent. Some way must be found, the defenders of the idea seem to say, to breach the limitations upon political action imposed by the existence of state sovereignty. The most important service yet performed by the demand for world government has been the focusing of popular attention upon the inadequacies of the present system. By a constant advocacy of extreme method of approach, the movement has made the less radical but nonetheless far-reaching measures of other types much more palatable to governments and peoples alike.

Regionalism: In considering supra-national organization a less-than-universal basis it is once again appropriate here to inquire into only one or two aspects of the question. Federation, either regional or functional, is most advanced in Europe, where the Schuman plan, the project for a European army, and the 1953 proposal for the political federation of six Western states has made the idea of a limited super-sovereignty a commonplace.

The citizens of Western Europe should be among the leaders in devising and seeking to implement schemes of supra-national organization. In Europe, people are keenly aware of the decline in the power and prestige of once great states, and are at every turn reminded of the obsolescence of the traditional state form. Nor do their problems any longer permit of effective unilateral action.

Furthermore, having passed through all the various phases of nationalism emotion, the no longer have the same degree of frantic attachment to the symbolism of the nation-state. No one can yet foresee the outcome of the European experiment in regional and functional federalism; at this point in history, however, one may be certain that the movement offers much hope and opportunity for real accomplishment and that it has already progressed too far to be lightly shrugged off.

Nationalist revivals may slow it down or halt its progress temporarily; the rivalry and ambitions of political leaders may obscure it; nevertheless, to millions of Europeans its attractions are so great that it must be given a complete and fair trial before they will agree to its abandonment.

The areas in which regional organization would appear to be appropriate include southeast Asia, the Middle East, Latin America. Natural functional groupings include the sugar-growing states of the world, the cotton-producing areas, and similar economic or social groupings. But throughout the remaining world there is not the willingness to dispense with rigid sovereign independence that one finds in Europe, because these peoples have not experienced the same events or suffered the same disillusionments, as have the Europeans. Independence is still too new and too precious to be lightly given up to a super-sovereignty. As a result, outside Europe most states are content today to seek organizational forms that preserve the complete identity of the nation-state.

Of the new forms of political organization the most numerous category is made up of the special-purpose organizations that preserve the essential characteristic of the state—national sovereignty. Generally these are created to serve a single purpose and are of limited jurisdiction and scope. In theory they are not different from any alliance between sovereignties; they are negotiated and take effect exactly in the same way as does any of the traditional forms of international agreement. Despite their external resemblances to the ordinary and familiar type of international instrument, however, closer examination of these new special purpose groupings reveals a fundamental difference in theory and in effect. In the first place, these groupings provide for much more intimate relationships than normally exists between sovereignties.

These special bodies serve to limit and weaken sovereignty by deriving a state of its former complete freedom of action in the area covered by the agreement. The foregoing points can perhaps be made more clear by reference to a few of these bodies. Perhaps the best known to Americans are the North Atlantic Treaty Organization (NATO) and the Organization of American States (OAS).

In Europe, among others are found the Organization for European Economic Co-operation (OEEC) and the European

Payments Union (EPU). Each of these bodies serves as the vehicle for closer co-operation on a more permanent basis than would be expected from a treaty relationship between sovereignties.

NATO

The NATO, an organization of fifteen European and North American states was created in 1949 to provide for mutual defense and joint action in case of attack. Other alliance of the past have had similar objective; what makes NATO unique is the degree of planning, close co-ordination, and tight integration that goes on with in the framework. No aspect of sovereignty is so central to statehood as control over one's own armed forces, yet there exists a permanent NATO armed force pledged to the collective defense of western Europe rather than to the mere protection of the homelands of the various members.

OEEC. The OEEC has in the same way served to merge the economies of the Western European states. Set up originally to carry out the European and of the *Marshall Plan of 1947* by creating ways for the European states to co-operate in their own economic recovery, it proved in practice to be an effective instrument. Its basic idea is the unity of the economy of Europe, and by promotion of intra-European trade and by channelling the flow of commodities into the states where they would be of the greatest value to recovery, it faciliated the most efficient utilization of the resources of the continent.

The work of the OEEC has progressed so far that the members find their economies closely integrated. Economic isolation for any of the OEEC countries, even if it were politically expedient, would be impossible without paying a tremendous cost in loss of production and a decline in the standard of living. When, after 1950, the purely economic aspect of American aid gave way to the concern with rearmament, the OEEC again was of great assistance in making possible the maximum effort by the various European states; it has thus served as a valuable adjunct to NATO.

As techniques mature and ramifications develop, the drift toward a more unified organization speeds up. The tendency in most of these special-purpose groups is toward federation or consolidation.

The Merger of Small States: A more specialized form of the flight from the nation-state is epitomized by the several instances when small states have merged their identities with those of other states, either joining larger one or assisting in the creation of an entirely new state. This is not yet a major trend but it is interesting and potentially important. It indicates a realization on the part of small states that no matter how great the joys of sovereignty may be, they are scarcely worth the price of tension and insecurity which they exact. By choosing membership in larger political community, the small states sacrifice complete self-determination but gain in return the greater protection and more solid economic foundation that flow from membership in the broader organization.

In 1948 the people of Newfoundland, offered a choice between self-government looking toward independence and membership in the Dominion of Canada, by popular vote chose the latter. Independence was less attractive than membership in a going concern. In the same way, federations are being planned for the British possessions in the Caribbean, and in 1953 an East African federation was created. More difficult to accomplish but perhaps more significant in the long run is the proposed political merger of the six Schuman Plan states of Europe.

Beginning with the customs union of the three low countries (Belgium, the Netherlands, and Luxembourg—known as 'Benelux') and spreading in many directions, by 1955 the movement had gained enough momentum.

This proposal does not contemplate a federation of limited scope; what it has in mind is the creation of a new political entity known simply as 'Europe.' Other such proposals are occasionally heard. The likelihood of their early adoption is not great, but they serve once again to underscore the need felt by peoples and governments for a base of political organization more efficient and rational.

Four centuries ago the state had a rational base as well: it represented the maximum area that could be efficiently governed from one seat. Today the technologies of peace and of war have made the old-style nation-state obsolete and impractical. We are in an age of giants, and the smaller states of the world are seeking to adjust themselves to the changed situation. They have attempted various techniques, as we have seen; all of them, however, eventually confront the immutable truth that the old state form upon which their organization is based cannot survive.

The time will come, and soon, when this realization will become general and what is now only a tendency will become a powerful force.

The whole framework of world politics will be altered to accommodate a society composed of fewer, although larger, members; even after this change takes place, however, the matter of rationalizing the relationships within the new community of large states will remain to be dealt with.

Legal, political, psychological, and emotional obstacles remain to be overcome before new and acceptable forms of organization are discovered. But that they well be found and put into operation is either a certainty or, at least, one of the major probabilities of the future.

IMPERIALISM ADIEU!

Once Europe became no longer a fertile field for imperial expansion because of its division into national states, the search for overseas empires was on. All the major states felt that their preferred status required the possession and exploitation of massive colonial possessions; many of the great international conflicts of recent history have hinged upon the possession of some colonial territory. Germany, Italy, and Japan—the late-comers upon the international scene—were driven to demanding and taking empires for themselves almost as soon as they had attained political maturity in the nineteenth century, even though most of the desirable territories of the world had already been appropriated and most of the other colonial powers had satiated themselves.

The United States, after a long quarrel with itself and its historical tradition, eventually succumbed; the end of the war with Spain in 1898 found the United States in possession of a far-flung empire in the Pacific and in the Caribbean. It can be fairly said that the pursuit and control of colonies was until recently a normal accompaniment of international politics.

Imperialism as a phenomenon has been analyzed often and there seems to be fairly general agreement that the empire-building urge was in most cases the result of a combination of motivations. Certain basic factors appear in nearly every instance of a policy of imperialism.

Security considerations have always been present and have often been paramount. States have sought colonies in order to secure advanced bases, strategic locations on communications routes, access to critical raw materials of strategic value, or sources of manpower.

Britain's empire was constructed for the most part with an eye to the value of the colony to a naval power; this explains the chains of British-controlled islands that extend across all of the oceans of the world.

France, on the other hand, made manpower an object of its colonialism: she exploited her African and Asiatic colonies to balance Germany's preponderance of population.

Economic reasons have also shaped many imperialist programmes. Marxist and Soviet theory makes this the entire explanation, purporting to discover an 'imperialist stage of capitalism,' when capitalist states are directed toward imperialism as a desperate last resort to stave off the imminent collapse of their system.

This argument, like so much communist theory, ignores both human psychology and recorded history and need not be taken seriously. Nevertheless, the search for raw materials and for controlled markets has frequently led states to adopt particular imperialist tactics, and economic motivations help explain much of imperialism.

The search for prestige has exerted much influence upon the imperialist drive. Possession of a colonial empire has been thought to make a state 'great' and to add several cubits to its stature. Imperial Germany demanded 'a place in the sun'—a colonial empire of its own—as a badge of its entry into the ranks of the great powers.

Most colonial empires were losing enterprises economically (the Dutch and Belgian were conspicuous exceptions) and instead of adding power they were usually sources of weakness because of the extensive dispersal of armed force they require and the constant danger of rebellion by the subject peoples. The rewards in prestige have usually been considered to be adequate by political leaders and peoples alike.

Of course, states and peoples were adept at concealing the real reasons for imperialism behind a wall of rationalizations. The usual form taken by this self-deception was that of stressing the 'civilizing' role of the imperialist power and asserting that in taking on the colony the state was only performing a duty of the highest importance. Britain cheerfully assumed the 'white man's burden' of freeing Asiatics and Africans from the bondage of slavery, savagery, and ignorance; France was proud of its *Mission civilatrice;* the Filipinos were the 'little brown brothers' of the Americans. The significance of missionary activity cannot be underestimated in this connection. There was no shortage of reasons to explain imperialism, whether one sought active motivations or moral justifications.

Salient Features of Imperialism: Eevery imperial power was unique in the way it approached the problem of governing its empire. Some were, in general, influenced for good upon the people of the colonies; others harmed their colonies more than they helped them. Some earned the bitter enmity of their subject peoples; others instead secured and retained a high degree of loyalty.

Certain fundamental similarities can be discovered in the way any imperialist power ruled its subject territories as yet.

Imperialism normally demanded that a colony be ruled in the interest of the mother country instead of in the interest of the residents of the territory. Empires were for the purpose of the aggrandizement of the homeland, and the lot of the colonial peoples was determined by what was good for the colonizer. Economic, cultural, political, and military policies were dictated by this common templation.

Economic exploitation was the rule rather than the exception. Whatever economic resources the territory offered were viewed as enriching the mother country, and little attempt was made to balance expenditures so as to equalize matters. Extractive natural wealth—mineral and agricultural—was usually exploited by a system of absentee landlordism, by the export of raw materials for processing elsewhere, and by the maintenance of a system of subsistence agriculture for the bulk of the native population. This pattern was followed regardless of the commodity involved; it was the same whether it was petroleum in the East Indies, diamonds in Africa, sugar in the Philippines, tin in Malaya, or rice in Myanmar.

The withholding of self-government from colonies and the granting of it only under extreme duress. Exceptions could be found—the policy of the United States in the Philippines is one—but self-government was generally regarded as a weakening of the imperial bond, and was resisted.

For a variety of reasons, some practical and others ideological, most imperialist powers felt impelled to import their own cultures into their colonies and, if need be, to destroy any competing native social order and value system.

Language, law, education, and religion alike were forcibly moulded into the image of the master people, and native organizational forms were either discouraged or forbidden. In Africa native tribal customs were frowned upon by Britain, France, Portugal, and Germany; in Asia, ancient civilizations, much older than those of their Western rulers, were crushed or driven underground.

Western claims to cultural superiority, tied in as they were with a complex of racial issues, ultimately created a heritage of bitterness which has made the adjustment of non-Western cultures to the remainder of the world most difficult.

The Eclipse of Old-Style Imperialism

The great colonial empires of the yore are gone, all postwar attempts of imperialist powers to retain colonial territories seeking independence having failed; in the truncated remnants of the old empires that remain, colonial policies are being undertaken that represent drastic revisions of earlier programmes.

Old-style imperialism has entered into its final fatal decline. What were the causes of this basic reversal of direction in the acquisition and rule of colonies?

One basic reason for the end of imperialism is the decline of the old imperial powers. The imperial giants of the pre-1914 world were Great Britain, France, the Netherlands, Belgium, and the

United States; the first three were the leaders both in the extent of territory ruled and their material wealth.

The power decline suffered by all the European powers made them incapable to rule and exploit these territories in anything like the manner of an earlier day. The states of Europe were so much occupied in maintaining their existence and independent status in a world growing steadily more unpropitious for them that they had progressively less and less power to spare for their empires. No colonial power ever dominated its empire by military strength alone, however. The technique of control used was compounded of a willingness to use unrestrained violence upon occasion and a bland assumption of superiority and the right to rule. This refusal even to consider any equity of treatment between homeland and colony usually left the native population baffled and unable to find any aperture in the wall of pride and prestige which the imperialist group built around themselves. Such native opposition as appeared was crushed ruthlessly. This fragile structure which supported imperialist rule in Asia, Africa, and other parts of the world crashed beyond repair during World War II. The Japanese, an Asiatic and non-white people, proved not only to Asiatics but to the entire world that white claims to superior power and ability were false.

The defeats inflicted upon the Allies in the Pacific in 1942 marked the end of an imperialist era. That the Japanese were finally defeated was immaterial; the damage to the colonial psychology was irreparable.

One of these disruptive forces went almost unsuspected until it broke with near-cataclysmic force. This was the fact that the native populations of the colonies, for many years deprived of most opportunities for self-advancement, had nevertheless profited greatly from their long and close association with Western technology.

In spite of their normally subordinate role in comparison with that of the imperial elite, they learned many valuable lessons from their contact with western learning and technology. Ironically enough, it was the very insistence of the colonial powers on the forced assimilation of Western culture that speeded up this process and made its eventual completion unavoidable.

Forced learning of Western languages proved profitable to

natives to profit from the wealth of scientific and humanistic data accumulated in the libraries and laboratories of the West. Once equipped with this information and made wiser by the insights it produced, the native populations of many colonial empires found themselves able to turn the resources of Western technology against their masters.

No doubt, the understanding of Western techniques and the capacity to employ them in the pursuit of nationalist objectives was confined to only a tiny portion of the native population of each territory, but this was the key group. Technicians in production and distribution were able to administer and build up the indigenous economy; specialists in political leadership were able to create formidable political groups by the employment of modern techniques of organization and mass communication. It is somewhat disconcerting to Western observers today to see the extent to which the former colonial peoples, intent on learning western methodology in order to gain self-determination, have copied the worst of the West as well as the best.

Economic exploitation is as unfair when carried on by a native group as when it is the practice of foreigners; corrupt political practices are as great a prostitution of democracy when done by former subjects as when done by imperialists.

The lesson is clear: the former colonial territories are thinking in terms of the future. They are still 'backward,' it is true, but they are now on the move toward the mastery and the manipulation of Western technology.

The Emergence of Nationalism: Imperialist techniques were effective only upon a non-political or apathetic population. As soon as the bulk of the people of any given areas came to share the mass emotion of nationalism, major revisions in the relationships between ruler and ruled became inevitable. Nationalism is mass movement; no elite, however constituted, can for long hold out against a population that is aware of its unity and is agreed in general terms upon its objectives. Once the peoples of the colonial areas went on the march, there was no longer any hope of saving the old system.

It has been since 1945 that the effect of colonial nationalism has been the most conspicuous. Colonial revolutions, violent and non-violent, have taken place in many subject territories in Asia and Africa. These have been generally successful in gaining complete or virtual independence when they have been backed by an aroused populace.

In some colonies, colonial powers have attempted to meet the demands of rising nationalism in order to stave off impending revolt. New policies have been inagurated which reverse earlier tactics and are aimed generally at granting more political autonomy and native self-determination.

In Central and South Africa, where the natives were organized on a tribal basis and live in a late Stone Age stage of development, the amount of opposition was meagre.

In North Africa and Middle East, social organization was somewhat more elaborate but the nomadic way of life of many of the people made it more difficult to develop a true mass resistance. In south and southeast Asia, where a large population with a complex culture was present in most of the colonized areas, opposition was at its greatest.

India's objections to its subordinate status dated from the appearance of British rule; the French had a constant struggle with native groups in Indo-China; the Dutch faced similar problems in the Indies. The opposition to imperial pretensions on the part of subject peoples is not a purely postwar condition.

Since 1945, native nationalism has grown stronger and has succeeded where formerly it had failed. In addition to the factors noted earlier, some additional reasons might be mentioned. In the aftermath of World War II there appeared a great wave of sympathy for all peoples struggling to be free. After a great victory over a foul tyranny it seemed to millions of people only just and fair that any group seeking independence should be granted it. This attitude was not confined to states without colonies of their own; sizable proportions of the population of each of the imperialist states were supporters of all movements for colonial independence, even those directed against their own government.

The effects of the war upon Asiatic imperialism were far-reaching. Not only did the Japanese victory over the white states serve to provide an example which others in Asia sought to emulate, but native nationalism received an opportunity to express itself during the struggle.

Different sorts of resistance movements existed in all the territories overrun by the Japanese, and these formed the nucleus of political organizations for independence and self-government at the end of the fighting.

By the time the Europeans arrived to resume control, the native governments were busy ruling their territories and were in no mood again to surrender control of their futures to alien hands. This situation occurred in Indonesia, in Burma, in Indo-China, in Malaya, and to some extent in the Philippines. The experience of independence and self-government provide the spark to native nationalism and all attempts to extinguish it were successfully prevented.

Another factor helping to explain the rise in colonial national spirit has been the improved communication within each area and between it and the rest of the world. This has meant that any successful revolt served as an example to all the others, and has intensified the movement everywhere. The colonial areas are no longer isolated; they are in contact with the United Nations and with groups of sympathizers everywhere, and each encourages the others.

The force of nationalism occasionally results in excesses; the strength of the emotion frequently obscures the vision and good judgment of the leaders of these groups, as in Iran and Myanmar.

The Future of Imperialism

Imperialism has no future; the day when great states could rule subject areas in blithe unconcern for any thing except the interest of the mother country has long since passed. It is self-evident, however, that there are yet millions of people in the world who are not prepared for self-government; to grant freedom immediately to all men everywhere would scarcely be doing them a kindness. When we realize this fact we see that for a long time to come many such areas must remain under the sponsorship and administration of some foreign country.

The Trusteeship Council and Article 73: The United Nations followed the example of the League of Nations and made national control over dependent and non-self-governing territories one of its matters of concern. In the United Nations system there are two areas of competence over colonial matters. In the first place, the Charter created a Trusteeship Council, which was to have jurisdiction over all trust territories for the ultimate disposition of which the organization has responsibility.

The Charter states: there are three types of trust territories: the surviving League of Nations mandates (largely German and Turkish territories stripped from the losers in World War I), territories detached from enemy states as a result of World War II (the colonial empires of Italy and Japan), and any territories voluntarily placed under the system by states responsible for their administration. Over these areas the United Nations through the Trusteeship Council has clear jurisdiction, and the state whose flag flies over them is merely a trustee.

The responsibility of the ruling state is clear; under the terms of the Charter it must govern the area with the primary purpose of promoting the 'political, economical, social, and educational advancement' of the people and their 'progressive development towards self-government or independence.' In other words, trust territories are not areas for economic exploitation or security planning; the rights of the inhabitants of the area are deemed to be dominant.

The Trusteeship Council has been successful in seeing to it that these obligations are carried out by the trustee powers. No greater reversal of traditional imperialist objectives could be imagined. The trusteeship system is of very limited application. The Charter also contains a statement of general colonial policy which is much broader in its scope and which foretells even more graphically that the trusteeship arrangement the future of colonial policy.

Article 73 of the Charter consists of a 'Declaration Regarding Non-Self-Governing Territories.' All members of the United Nations who 'have or assume responsibilities for the administration of territories whose peoples have not yet attained a full measure of self-government' now admit the principle that 'the interests of the inhabitants of these territories are paramount' and agree to make this the guiding notion of their governance.

Many specific obligations are accepted by each colonial state, including principally the insuring of the advancement of the people, the development of self-government and the transmission regularly to the Secretary-General of information about the manner and the extent to which each of them is honouring its pledge.

No coercive method is prescribed to enforce this declaration except that of publicity and public opinion. Yet the implications of this declaration are of enormous scope. At the time of its signature all the colonial powers of the meant that all the non-self-governing areas of the world would thenceforth be ruled in the primary interest of their inhabitants.

New Colonial Policies: In general they all aim at the implementation of Article 73, although the speed and the specific details obviously very in each case, depending upon local conditions and the particular situation of the ruling power.

United Kingdom, with the most extensive empire in the world, has undertaken a many-sided programme of fostering the development of its dependent peoples and speeding the transition toward self-government. Learning its lesson from the loss of India and Burma, it has instituted fundamental reforms in virtually all its possessions. Since 1945 it has initiated project of federation that will grant political autonomy for its Caribbean possessions and for its East African territories. In those areas—such as the Gold Coast—where native development has proceeded far enough, it has established native legislatures and administrations.

In the more backward areas it has deliberately sought to encourage there development of native culture with a judicious admixture of Western technology; while sponsoring the growing self-discovery of the natives it also assists in the introduction of modern techniques of public health, communications, and government.

After making allowance for the unevenness of any democratically determined policy of this sort, Britain's record in the execution of the obligations it assumed under Article 73 compares favourably with that of any other state, and it seem sincerely interested in moving its dependent peoples toward genuine self-government as rapidly as their development permits.

France has had a more stormy time in its colonial adventure since 1945 than Britain. It has had to contend with a long and expensive colonial war in Indo-China (and eventually lost at least half the territory) and with riots and outbreaks in North Africa. Its internal political instability has also deprived it of the continuity in policy which is necessary for an orderly transition from an old era to a new.

In its Central African colonies, a new paternalism has to some extent replaced the more distant rule of another day. A much greater degree of official concern now exists for the welfare of the natives in such matters as health, education, and economic status. There is a notable difference between the French and the British policies, however. The French view the development of the natives toward self-government as possible only through a continually closer approximation of France itself; the progress of the people is to take place through a greater assimilation of French culture.

The Netherlands lost much of its empire with the successful revolt of Indonesia. It has attempted, in that portion left to it, to prevent further defections by following a more enlightened programme.

Belgium, with most of its empire concentrated in one great area in Central Africa, the Congo, has not had major native movements to contend with has sought to prevent them by revising its policy in the general direction of native improvement; the great profit accruing to the home government from the colony make sufficient funds available for the purpose.

Some people speak of the Congo as the 'garden colony' of Africa. Spain and Portugal have not made any great change in their colonial administrations; Portugal's record is the better of the two. As a result colonial problems are building up which these states will be called upon to deal with in the future.

Ultimately, the United States is also moving with great rapidity toward self-government for its dependent possessions. Philippine independence was a promise before World War II; it has been a reality since 1946. Puerto Rico has acquired the status of a 'commonwealth' with complete autonomy, and in 1953 President Eisenhower offered it complete independence.

New States' Role

Their behaviour has demonstrated certain common characteristics derived largely from their recently acquired independence, and although all will undoubtedly become more and more aware of the responsibilities attendant upon sovereign status, at the present time they tend to produce problems of a unique sort.

Certain ingredients appear in the policies of all these new states. Perhaps the most pervasive is anti-colonialism. Acutely conscious of their own independence and the struggle most of them passed through in order to achieve it, they assume the role of liberators of all peoples remaining under alien rule anywhere. This necessitates the active or passive support of all independence movements in colonial areas and constant agitation before world public opinion in favour of these groups. It also makes necessary hostility toward all colonial powers, particularly their own former rulers.

This opposition is not retrained to colonial questions but often extends into other policy areas as well. In the United Nations the new states are constantly urging an extension of the trusteeship system and exert great pressure on the colonial power in the direction of greater implementation of Article 73. A second common characteristic is neutralism, actual or attempted. We have already discussed the tendency of many states to deal that the cold war is no concern of theirs and to seek to insulate themselves from it. This is particularly true of most of the new states. They seek not only to avoid involvement in the quarrel but to conduct relations with both sides with studied impartiality.

They also display a third common approach to policy: self-assertiveness. They uniformly resist any proposal from any quarter that smacks of coercion in any form; they insist upon the most literal respect for their complete independence. Their recent non-self-governing status is fresh in their minds and they are intensely aware of the symbolism of sovereignty. As a result they are often accused of being uncooperative and belligerent.

Another point upon which they generally agree is strong support of the United Nations.

Distrusting the bipolar blocs as being potentially accuse for way, they place their faith and their trust in the United Nations instead. Only in collective guarantees of security can the safety of small states be found.

Excessively nationalistic and intent on playing a major role in world affairs, the new states at the present time constitute something of a special problem for all the other states. The direction of their future development depends to a considerable extent upon the course followed by their nationalism.

If it follows the example of Europe, for an indefinite time in the future the new states will continue to be xenophobic and unco-operative, and they will recede from this extreme position only by learning as the result of war and devastation that sovereign independence is not the greatest of all joys.

If, on the other hand, the new states are able to profit by the example of others and can absorb the lessons of the interdependence of peoples and the ultimate futility of unilateral nationalism without passing through the disillusionments themselves, their concern with peace and security may well make them leaders in the drive to create a worldwide system of guarantees.

The question will be answered in terms of the attitude and policy of other states during the present period of transition. This is of primary importance to the United States, since we are vigorously interested in such an era of peace and stability.

If American policy is patient and forbearing, if we so not indulge the temptation to employ our superior strength to coerce these smaller states, if instead we take account of their foibles and make allowances for their inexperience and the powerful emotions to which they are subject, the opportunity for winning them over to a co-operative attitude is great.

The case of India is particularly pertinent. India, as the United States has already learned to its discomfiture, simply will not submit to coercion, even in its own interest. Instead, the Indian government has demonstrated a great eagerness to learn from the West and to work as an equal partner for common security.

5

Concept of National Policy

National (also called external) policy may be defined as the overall course of action taken by a state in seeking to attain its national objectives. The essential ingredient in policy is, thus, action directed toward a discernible goal.

International politics, thus, arises out of the contacts that states have with each other as each of them pursues its policy. Relatively little in interstate relations is entirely fortuitous; international intercourse, conflict, and agreement grow out of purposeful behaviour by governments. The adjustment of policy to meet the requirements of a constantly changing situation is the continuing task of a statesman. In attempting to attain his policy objectives he must apply both his insight into the nature of world politics and his skill in manipulating men and circumstances.

NATIONAL INTEREST

The concept of interest is basic to international politics. Because of its identity with deeply felt and often inarticulate national aspiration of a people it is difficult to isolate and to define with precision.

Commonly, it may be thought of us as that which a state and its people feel to be permanently essential to continued national existence and development. It gains its specific details in terms of the ego-image which a people have of themselves. It embodies either those aspects of national existence which the group possesses and insists upon retaining or those it lacks and aspire for to acquire.

Nature and Source of National Interest: National interest arises out of the interaction of a number of factors whose precise effect varies from state to state; geographic and strategic position; the level of political, economic and social development; national history, tradition, and culture; the over-all Weltanschauung of the people.

If states are thought of as living entities possessed of unique personalities, it follows that they have reasons for existence and specific goals to reach; in other words, they possess interests. The hopes and objectives of individuals become sublimated into a common pattern within the state.

National interest is the state's interest and is, thus, divorced from any necessary connection with the interests of any particular individual or group. Furthermore, since today 'state morality'—the ethical code in terms of which state action is judged—is independent of private morality, the service of the national interest is for private citizens an act of great virtue.

There arises at this point a real possibility of conflict. Individuals are often required, while serving in a public role, to commit acts which their private code condemns as immoral. Such conflicts in individual motivation are, therefore, relatively uncommon. Statesmen are able to count upon the idea of national interest as an effective device to gain popular support for their policy decisions.

The national interest of a state remains operative despite change in any or all the circumstances of its foreign policy. It is independent of the internal political struggle within a government and is not affected by the policies of other states. The idea of national interest and its impact upon the course of events furnishes a regularizing and continuing factor in international affairs. Many dramatic examples of this continuity can be provided. The government of the Iran, Soviet Union, for example, has lately reverted to the Czarist idea of Russian national interest despite many attempts to tread upon a new path. The Labour government of Great Britain which was elected in 1945, although pledged to thoroughgoing social revolution at home, nevertheless picked up the threads of British national interest abroad and carried on in much the same way as had its Conservative predecessor. In like fashion the electoral reverse of 1952 which returned the Conservatives under Sir Churchill produced no significant change in British interest. A change in party control in the United States, such as that which occurred in 1952, sometimes has greater repercussion in foreign policy than is the case in Britain.

In spite of the relative permanence of the idea of national interest, it must not be assumed that it remains immune forever to change. Since the prevailing version of national interest at any time is really a product of cultural and political outlook of a people, one would expect cultural, economic, political, and psychological evolution to produce corresponding development in this idea of national interest, and this is actually the case. The modifications of the prevailing American notion of security as an element in the national interest is illustrative. A century ago, security to the American people involved only United States hegemony over the Western hemisphere.

Certainly history offers many examples of interests that have broadened in their expression over a long period, and not a few of interests that have contracted.

Significance of National Interest: Most of the people themselves are unaware of the particular version of national interest which they share, or else several different interpretations are competing for group acceptance.

The elusiveness of the concept of interest in no way minimizes its key role in national policy. A statesman must be sensitive to the state of mind of his people and seek to base his decisions upon what they regard as national interest. This is a formidable task—to know a people sometimes better than they know themselves—but it is one of the primary requirements of political leadership. Policy makers can do very little about altering the prevailing concept of interest; the best they can do is to have always a clear picture of what it is and to see to it that they do not depart from it in making decisions.

Policy: As Manifestation of Interest

As national interest is the foundation upon which a statesman must build in seeking the achievement of his objectives, he must follow a fairly standard procedure. He must first translate the general idea of national interest into solid terms and formulate a series of policy objectives; then, he selects techniques appropriate to the attainment of these goals. This is the policy process pure and simple. In framing policy, the statesman begins with two constants and many variables. The constants are the existence of the national interest he is expected to serve, and the existence of other states, each likewise pursuing its own policy. The variables include all the possible policy objectives deriving from his state's national interest, all the techniques available to him for reaching these objectives, and the many forms that the policies of other states might take.

Policy Decision: The process by which a policy decision is made has been fairly well standardized in most states. Statesmen, are faced with a constantly evolving situation with which they must attempt to cope. The impact of developing circumstances upon national interest is always being evaluated; whenever action in its behalf become appropriate, policy decision must be made. When the responsible official of a government become convinced that measures must be taken to guard or promote the national interest, their first step is to make as thorough and objective an analysis of the situation as is probable.

When this process is completed and all the alternatives and their likely results are examined, a choice is made among them. That policy is selected which promises the most gain to the national interest, and steps appropriate to its accomplishment are, then, undertaken. This summary of the policy process is somewhat oversimplified, but it is accurate in its essentials. So long as statesmen feel themselves obliged to serve the national interest exclusively and as long as the nation-state system imposes its peculiar requirements upon the foreign policies of states, the policy process will continue to be approached as a problem in determining that course of action which will redound to the greatest benefit to the state itself. Since policy decisions must be made every time a situational change occurs, and since the circumstances upon which decisions are based in a state of constant flux, it follows that any state which seeks to play an active international role must be always overhauling its policy.

Limitations on Policy Decisions

It should be pointed out at this point, however, that the policy-making process does not in practice go forward with as much freedom of choice as might be inferred from the foregoing analysis.

The statesman usually finds the realistic alternatives open to him in any situation to be extremely limited. It is to his advantage, of course, to preserve the maximum freedom of manoeuver, but he is always faced with many factors over which he has little or no control. He is in the first place confined by the prevailing concept of the national interest, which he must respect. Second, he is to a great extent bound by earlier commitments, the revocation of which is almost difficult and is often impossible. Any policy maker must move with great caution in attempting to alter policies which his government has had under way for a long time and which it supports with considerable power. International disturbances of unsuspected proportions might develop from any such new departure. Any policy shift might produce a chain reaction of adjustment to it on the part of other states.

One more limiting factor upon policy choice arises from the nature of international relations. A statesman is more than a framer and executor of policy aimed at satisfying the national interest of his state; he is also the subject of pressure from other governments seeking to accomplish the same purpose on their own part. Policy makers, therefore, often spend as much effort in reacting to moves aimed at themselves by other states as they do in seeking to achieve their own aims.

Operational Criteria

Certain operational criteria affect all policy decisions. The primary fact that any objective selected must be intelligible in terms of the national interest has already been established.

The objective and the programme for its attainment must also be stipulated in concrete terms. Nothing is so self-defeating, for an individual as well as for a state, as to pursue an objective couched in hazy and imprecise phraseology.

Much efforts committed to the search after a will-o-the-wisp that constantly recedes as it is approached. Such objectives as 'peace under the law' or 'an end to imperialism' tend to involve the state in a maze of inconclusive policies which can never be rationalized or completed.

What we are actually saying is that objectives and policies formulated in concrete terms and based upon actual situation are almost always relative in character and take into account the existence of other states and other competing policies. In those terms it becomes clear that a state must always content itself with something less than complete victory.

Policy, if its ends are to be accomplished, must enumerate specific goals in relation to real states and situations, and, then, follow courses of action which arise from those realities.

Policy objectives must also be attainable. A state must seek to avoid biting off more than it can chew. No matter how insistent the promptings of national interest, it would be unwise for the government of a small state, such as Nicaragua or Burma, to undertake a policy looking toward the attainment of world domination. A rational statesman always keeps in mind the maximum effort he would be willing or able to make in support of any of his policies, and seeks to keep his selection of objectives within those limits.

Big states have collapsed as a result of seeking an objective that demanded more effort for its attainment than they were capable of mustering.

A policy must also be flexible. No area of human activity is more subject to sudden change than is international affairs, owing to the basically irresponsible nature of the state. The arena in which any state moves is one of great confusion of motivation, and a process of constant adjustment to the rapidly changing situation is going on. A policy decision is reached as a result of the application of a concept of national interest to a particular situation, the choice of appropriate objectives, and the selection of expedient means. The decision is affected by such factors as the relations the state is maintaining with all other states, the attitude of all other states toward the problem under consideration, and the general pattern of world politics. Any one of these may and probably will change momentarily. A policy that assumes the indefinite continuation of the *status quo* is doomed to futility and failure. No more common fault can be found of political leadership in the contemporary world. Many of the international crises and wars that beset mankind could have been avoided if policy makers had recognized the possibility that conditions might arise that would make their assumptions invalid and their policy inappropriate. To assume that because a state has done thus-and-so in the past it will continue to do so is to assume that all the complex factors that produced the policy in the first place will continue to exert their influence in exactly the same manner.

Flexibility in policy is best attained by directing the state's course of action toward the accomplishment of a series of alternative objectives, with the final selection among them being determined by the changing situation. Whenever possible, statesmen embark upon a new departure in policy somewhat tentatively, hoping to verify the accuracy of their preliminary judgments before irrevocably committing themselves.

The inevitable situation of pressure opposed by counter-pressure which every state faces in international politics is such that only rarely will a policy result in exactly the outcome envisaged at the time of its inception. The dynamic quality of interstate relations requires that every state be constantly busy adjusting its policy.

Types of National Policies

Though many elaborate schemes have been drawn up to develop a system by which classify the foreign policies of various states, the pattern of international politics is so variable that it resists simplification. It has also proved difficult to avoid an excess of moral judgment in establishing criteria.

Actually, there is only one criterion that can be successfully applied to the foreign policies of all states with any real result, and the classification is, therefore, a dual one. The standard of measurement is the state's attitude and policy toward the over-all *status quo* which it faces. Although many fine distinctions can be drawn within each group, a state's policy either reflects a general satisfaction with things as they are or else fundamental discontent.

States of the first group are termed 'satiated' or 'have' powers; states of the second are dubbed 'revisionist' or 'have-not' powers. It must be noticed that the 'have' or 'have-not' situation of a state depends not upon the attainment or non-attainment of any absolute level of security or standard of living, but rather upon its attitude toward that level which it has attained. In the postwar world the Soviet Union, despite its relatively favourable position in relation to most of the other states of the world.

POLICY FORMULATIONS

It is appropriate at this point to examine in more detail the process of decision making in order to make clear who these individuals actually are and the role each plays.

Officials Directly Concerned

By and large international politics tends to be a function of executive officers and heads of states. International law today retains the anachronistic fiction that the interstate relations are personally carried on by the various heads of state. This is literally true only in special cases in the modern world, but the executive branch retains its dominant role.

In addition to the pervasive force of custom, two factors help explain the predominance of executive over legislative departments in the field of foreign policy.

In the process of conducting foreign affairs these officials gain the detailed and technical information upon which alone intelligent policy decisions can be based.

Foreign policy calls for the exercise of strong political leadership for which only executive officers are qualified. Legislatures (in those states in which an independent legislature exists under a theory of separation of powers) are also handicapped by the lack of machinery under their direct control which might be employed to implement any decisions they might reach on their own.

The Chief Executive: Within the executive branch of the government most states have a roughly similar arrangement for foreign affairs. The operating head of the state—the chief executive—still retains the key role in decision making, whether he be president, prime minister, or dictator. Although in practice he usually confines himself to broad policy consideration, leaving the detailed implementation of decisions to technically trained subordinates, the nature of his position is usually such as to give him as much personal power in matters of foreign policy as he cares to exercise. Direct negotiations between heads of governments has been a relatively uncommon occurrence, although several centuries ago it was a normal channel of international intercourse.

Although not taking place under such dramatic circumstances since the war until Geneva in 1955, face-to-face relations between chief executives is no longer regarded as unusual in interstate negotiation. During the more acute stages of the cold war, between 1948 and 1952, there were many suggestion heard on both sides of the Iron Curtain that only by another round of top-level conferences between the opposing leader could major progress toward the easing of the tension be accomplished. This demand for face-to-face diplomacy was intensified following the death of Stalin early in 1953. In 1955 the United States agreed to a renewal of top-level talks with the then USSR.

As a routine matter, however, the chief executive today permits the determination of day-to-day policy to rest in the hands of his subordinates, reserving his own activity to crisis situations or the establishment of broad policy principles.

The Foreign Office

1. *The Foreign Minister*—Directly concerned with foreign policy in every state is the executive department of foreign affairs. The foreign minister, the administrative chief of this department (his formal title varies, of course, from government to government), usually bears the greatest burden on decision making on foreign affairs in the entire governmental structure. His relation to his chief (the chief executive) is an elastic one, depending upon the personalities involved and the constitutional arrangements of the particular government. In any case, the decisions that fall to him to make are peculiarly difficult. He works within the broad policy framework of his government (in the shaping of which he may have had only a small part, or none at all) and deals with the questions that transcend routine, either because of their scope or because of their inherent difficulty.

He is required to combine insight and judgment with great administrative ability, because in addition to his policy-making function he normally oversees the execution of all the diplomatic procedures of his government.

2. *Home Personnel*—Within the cabinet department of foreign affairs are two groups, each of which plays a major role in policy making. The first is the home personnel of the department who

direct the detailed activities of the overseas diplomatic corps and receive their reports. Here is a repository of specialized knowledge of particular areas and problems which does not exist at higher levels. In the course of the performance of their fairly routine task, many policy decisions are made by this group. These decisions are not sufficiently important in themselves to merit being referred to higher-ranking personnel but in the aggregate they constitute a major portion of a state's policy. The influence of these near-anonymous bureaucrats is almost ignored by the public, but statesmen are acutely aware of it. The larger the organization state has for the conduct of foreign affairs, the greater the part these people play in its determination.

In some ways this is unfortunate; in the execution of their functions, these lower-echelon officials develop precedents and commitments that are difficult to modify if the need to do so should arise. In this way, the decisions by the home personnel of the foreign office constitute one of the more stable elements in the policy of a state, although it must be admitted that this is often to its detriment.

3. *The Diplomatic Corps*—The other significant group in the department of foreign affairs is, of course, the diplomatic corps of a state. The improvements in transportation and communication of recent times have made it possible for governments today to remain in intimate contact with their diplomats abroad and to direct their activities much more closely than was formerly the case. This has resulted in a great diminution in the range of discretionary action and consequently in the immediate importance of the diplomat in decision making. Most governments carry on fairly close 'back-seat driving' of their representative abroad.

Not only has the day-by-day role of the diplomat been reduced; in time of crisis, it is likely that affairs will be taken completely out of his hands by a meeting of foreign ministers, special emissaries or chief executives.

The duties of a diplomat are three: representation, negotiation, and the gathering and report of information. Particularly, in the last function is his role critical. By the selection and evaluation of the data he forwards to his home government he can so influence the thinking of the high-level decision makers as practically to stack the cards in favour of the policy he personally prefers.

Officials Less Directly Concerned

1. *The Cabinet*: Outside the foreign-affairs department itself in almost all states are several agencies that share in the policy process. Of these the most influential is often the cabinet or the corresponding body of general advisor to the chief executive.

The foreign minister is himself a member of the cabinet and plays a leading part in its discussion of foreign affairs, but to varying degrees the entire body enters into the making of policy. Its usual mission is that of recommending broad policies to the chief executive, often approving or modifying projects that arise in the first instance with the foreign minister. The cabinet members bring to this task the point of view of foreign affairs non-specialists.

Cabinet recommendations often ignore situational aspects of a problem which might make their proposed policy inexpedient or impossible, but they sometimes (particularly in a democracy) display greater insight into the domestic implications of foreign policy than do the more specialized recommendations of the foreign minister.

2. *Minister Personnel*—It is obvious that military considerations be given much weight in arriving at a policy decision. The exact importance assumed by military personnel in the hierarchy of policy makers within a government is a question answerable only in terms of the political dynamics of the state concerned. A distinction may be drawn, however, between those states that view the military establishment as a servant of national interest and those that consider military power its determinant.

The latter tend to make military considerations paramount in their calculations; the former restrain it to a role more auxiliary in character. Military men, in general, make their decisions and recommendations in terms of two variables: the impact of the proposed policy upon the military security of their state, and the military feasibility of the proposed steps.

3. *Non-Foreign Affairs Bureaucracy*—The non-foreign affairs bureaucracy of a state also participates in the policy process. To understand the role of this group one must keep in mind the peculiar processes of the bureaucratic mind. Each agency of a government is staffed by individuals who feel quite sincerely that the destiny

of their government is bound up with the success of their particular goal.

Informal and Unofficial Decision-Makers

Many other individuals participate in the dynamic process of reaching a foreign-policy decision. All of them in some way influence the responsible officials whose actions alone will give content to policy conclusions. It is difficult in event the most favourable circumstances to determine beyond question the factors that influenced any individual statesman to choose one course of action over another.

Political parties, however, organized and directed, obviously embody forces that play in foreign policy. A distinction must be drawn between the parties of a democratic state and those monolithic mass movements which are such a familiar appurtenance of dictatorial governments today. Democratic parties represent the most politically active segments of a population and, therefore, are thought of as peculiarly reliable barometers of public opinion. In a democracy executive officers, including those charged with foreign affairs, are also party members and the opinions of the party leadership cannot help but be given weight by office holders. In such states as France and United States, party politics often serves as one of the real determinants of foreign policy.

Totalitarian parties are organized upon a different theory from democratic ones, being instruments of popular control rather than channels by which public opinion may be translated into governmental action.

The totalitarian party in a dictatorship is in many ways even more important to foreign policy than is its democratic counterpart. Since government is a party monopoly in such a state as the then USSR, this means that all government decisions are in the first instances taken within party leadership circles. The policy of the Soviet government is first and foremost the policy of the Russian Communist Party; the same was true in Nazi Germany.

Pressure groups constitute another important segment of the unofficial decision-making elements in a population. Their effect is confined for the most part to states within the orbit of Western culture, since outside it conditions are not propitious for the formation of private groups that attempt to influence government action in the direction they advocate.

Each new crisis in world affairs seems to be the signal for the creation of a number of organizations that seek to produce governmental action favouring their particular side of the case.

Of all the unofficial elements in the policy process, perhaps, the most difficult upon which to be specific is the shadowy role played by private individuals. No statesman confines his friendships to members of his official family, and whenever any individual stands in such relation to a policy maker as to be privy to his thoughts and capable of influencing his decisions, such a relationship cannot help but determine policy.

Often the general public is unaware of the extent to which private citizens such as these are influencing the determination and conduct of foreign policy, and no one except the men concerned can ever be certain of the importance of such a relationship.

Public opinion the final ponderable in the policy process. Since popular sentiment embodies the prevailing concept of the national interest, and since any war today must command popular support to be successful, every statesman makes a constant effort to keep his policy in line with public opinion.

Often a totalitarian ruler stands in greater fear of popular disaffection than does a popularly elected chief executive. If the latter flouts public opinion in his foreign policy, the worst that can normally happen as a result is the loss of his position and personal power; if a dictator violates the wishes of his people he runs the danger of destroying his regime and possibly losing his life. However, to base one's policy upon national interest is expressed in public opinion is one thing; to do nothing but pander to popular prejudice is another, and a very much worse thing.

The rational statesman is aware of the attitudes of his people and is responsive to them, but at the same time he is constantly leading and educating them to an awareness of the responsibilities of foreign policy.

The Internal Struggle over Policy: The foregoing enumeration of the several participants in the policy process naturally raises the question of how decisions are actually arrived at among the many conflicting recommendations advanced. It seems to be true in all states that a struggle generally takes place among the would-be architects of policy, both official and unofficial, before most final decisions are reached. The controversy may be of long duration or it may be brief; it may involve the general public or it may be waged behind the closed doors of government.

It may be rooted in domestic political considerations or it may grow out of foreign relations pure and simple. Its ultimate outcome is determined by the relative strengths of the participants and the political arrangements of the state involved. Further generalization about the nature of this recurrent phenomenon is not possible, except to repeat that few, if any, states are able to reach important policy decisions without first becoming involved in, and resolving, such an internecine quarrel.

Objectives of Policy

It is, of course, impossible to establish a single catalogue of the policy objectives sought by all states. The course of action followed by any state arises from circumstances peculiar to itself, and no two national policies are alike.

No state necessarily seeks all of these simultaneously, and each state gives each category specific content and arranges them in priority as determined by circumstances. The listing that follows serves only to point out the frequently broad objectives that regularly appear in the policies of all states.

Self-preservation as an objective connotes, of course, much more than continuation of national existence, although on occasion it may be reduced to nothing more than that.

States seek to avoid being placed in a position that might endanger or reduce their capacity to exist. Two major sub-categories of self-preservation might be mentioned separately: territorial-integrity and political independence.

States accept as axiomatic the idea that the national territory is inviolate and no part of it is to be alienated except under extreme duress, most frequently encountered following military defeat. Once territory has been lost, or when the state feels that it does not possess certain territory that rightfully belongs to it, the acquisition of that territory becomes major objective of foreign policy. This is sometimes known as 'irredentism'. Territorial integrity is a universal and frequently obsessive of the foreign policies of contemporary states.

Political independence is frequently insisted upon as well. Since the legal concept of sovereignty is so vigorously buttressed today by the energizing force of nationalism, it is to be expected that a state would make every effort to avoid being brought under another state's political control, and would make an ever greater effort once again to escape from it if such should occur.

States conduct their policies so as to remain the maximum freedom of choice under all circumstances and no state willingly accepts subordination to another except, in return, for concrete advantages in another area of national interest. Particularly are states jealous of their internal sovereignty. The jurisdiction of a state within its boundaries is claimed to be absolute, and what takes place within its borders felt to be the business of no other government. Independence in this sphere is felt to be the *sine qua non* of national existence.

Security

The international society is one in which states must constantly be on the alert against the possibility of attack by another state. This situation gives rise to another virtually universal category of policy objective, that of security. All states make a real effort to achieve it. So pervasive is its influence that modern international politics has often been summed up as 'the search for security'.

The concept of security is another of the elusive realities of international politics. It originates in the group attitudes of the people of a state and can best be comprehended in psychological terms. Security is a condition in which a people need not and do not fear a successful attack upon them by any combination of forces. Viewed in this light, absolute security can be attained by a state only when it has under its direct control a great preponderance of the total power of the world.

Empirically, any state that attempted to become secure by means of world hegemony would probably meet such resistance almost from the very inception of such a policy as to dissipate the security it was already enjoying.

As a rule, states today recognize the unattainability of absolute security. Instead of following the futile course of guarding against all possible enemies, they attempt to organize their policies so as to reduce the danger of a successful attack to the practical minimum.

This approach to security necessitates initially an evolution of the situation in terms of the more probable sources of attack. In making this judgment, a statesman estimates the international conflicts engendered by his policy, the states with which he is in disputes, and the probable severity of their reactions.

In this manner, the search for security is resolved into two parts; first, the protection of the minimum requirements of national existence (a continuing problem which is independent of other aspects of policy); second, the taking of measures to cope with expected dangers arising out of the implementation of deliberate policy steps.

A state playing a lone hand in this regard must also utilize its diplomacy in such fashion as to prevent there being ranged against it a bloc of states with greater aggregate. States prefer to do as much of this as they can by themselves, because in return for the increase of strength which arises from the conclusion of an alliance they must forego a certain amount of their freedom of choice and action. It is only the exceptional state, however, that is able to dispense with international arrangements to guarantee its own security, and various forms of alliances, ententes, and 'understandings' for a common security purpose are common. These take two forms: either they are non-aggression treaties whereby each party remove itself as security threat to the other's by promising not to attack it in return for a similar guarantee from the other signatories; or else they are mutual-defense agreements, in which several states that feel themselves menaced by the same security threat agree to put their strength against the common aggressor.

In the modern world the Locarno Pact of 1925, in which France and Germany agreed not to go to war over the issue of the western boundary of Germany, provides one of the most illustrious examples of a non-aggression treaty; the North Atlantic Security Pact of 1949 which tied the United States, Canada, and the states of Western Europe into a common alliance against Soviet aggression is perhaps the most famous contemporary mutual security arrangement.

Collective Security: To provide a more stable basis for international relations, the twentieth century has seen a continuous effort to make vital the concept of 'collective security'. If every state, the world, or at least a great majority of them, realized the universal urgency of the question of security, the whole problem could be nearly resolved by each state's guaranteeing every other state's security.

Thus, if any state's policy led it to the point of menacing world peace and the security of any other individual state, the remainder of the states of the world would range themselves against the disturber of the peace with such preponderance of power that no same statesman would risk a war. At one stroke the age-old problem of security would be solved. The idea, within rallying cry, 'peace is indivisible', underlay the League of Nations and implicit in the peace-enforcing activities of the United Nations.

The arrival of a crisis produced mixed reaction among the states of the world; instead of the great bulk of power being aligned against the disturber of the peace, part of it was supporting the aggressor, part was following the policy of 'hands off', and only a portion was defending the principle.

Case of Korea: This was clearly the situation that followed the most ambitious attempt to implement the principle, the United Nations intervention into the Korean crisis in 1950. One sizable power bloc, the Soviet world, pointedly ignored the United Nations and extended covert assistance to aggressors.

Another, the so-called 'neutral', led by India, expressed guarded approval of the action by the organization, but refrained from assisting in any way to carry it out. The third, and numerically the largest, group was led by the United States. It gave active military support to the attempt to apply collective force to restrain the enemy.

Regional Collective Security Agreements

Many regional collective-security arrangements have been somewhat more successful. Both in the Western Hemisphere (the Organisation of American States) and in other areas (the North Atlantic Treaty Organization and ANZUS—the United States-Australia-New Zealand alliance), such geographically limited alliance guarantee the security of the membership as regards aggression both from outside and from each other.

Collective Economic Advantage

States commonly have economic objectives included as part of their foreign policies. These economic goals are usually related to the economic advantage of the state and the people collectively and therefore they bear no necessary relationship to the gain or loss to any or all individuals.

For example, stockpiling rare raw materials may free the national economy from dependence upon foreign sources of supply and thus be advantageous to the state, but stockpiling is an expensive business and the result to individuals would be an increase in taxes and in the cost of the commodities produced with the stockpiled materials. Thus an added inconvenience would be placed upon citizens without any corresponding personal gain in return. If the programme under consideration is desirable from the point of view of the national interest, it is undertaken. Perhaps in no other area is the conflict between national (state) interest and private interest so frequent and so obvious as in economic policy.

Importance of Economic Objectives: It was previously quite common to assign economic objectives first place in the priority of the policy objectives of states. To this point of view international relation, like all other forms of politics, was a manifestation of economic determinism, and all affairs was deemed to be a struggle for raw materials, markets, and productive capacity.

Today we can admit that economic factor play a significant role in the determination of the policy objectives of states, and that at a given time and for particular state they may be primary, without proceeding then to argue the all international contacts reflect nothing but the clash of economic interest. Only Marxist analysis retain their rigidly determinist position, and their point of view is seriously compromised by the attendant paraphernalia communist dialectic.

Protection and Promotion of Economic Interest: The protective aspect of economic policy takes many forms in the contemporary world. Some of the more common ways include the protection of the domestic price level by means of a protective tariff, the protection of the wage level by restrictive and selective immigration policies, the retention within the country of critical material and products by export controls, as the protection of the national monetary system by exchange limitations. Protection can be carried to the extreme by the policy objective which establishes as a goal the complete freedom of the state from economic dependence upon the outside world.

Economic objectives of the latter sort are often particularly emphasized in the policy of a 'revisionist' or 'have-not' state.

Raw Materials: Some further attention must be paid to one great economic objective mentioned above. In a world grown industrialized, certain critical raw materials have become essential to the maintenance of a technology adequate to support great national power.

As these main raw materials are as distributed evenly throughout the globe but are concentrated in a relatively small number of locations, the search for guaranteed access to sources of their supply is an unending process for most states.

As each major change in technology has taken place since early in the eighteenth century, different raw materials have, each in its, become critical. As each one of them became of matter of importance, it served to touch off anew the scramble among the states for a guaranteed supply.

Today the great prize is petroleum, accompanied since World War II by the global search for source of nuclear fuels. Any further technological revolution would produce still another battle for control of any new critical material. Recent US invasion of Iraq is evidence of this.

A state involved in this struggle—as almost all of them are–seeks initially to discover adequate resources located within its borders, either by discovery within its historic frontiers or by the annexation of new territory containing sufficient resources endowment.

This was substantially the procedure adopted by the government of the United States as it sought to guarantee itself sufficient raw materials for atomic bombs. Ultimately, the United States was forced to come to an almost pre-emptive purchase agreement with Belgium with regard to the Uranium deposits in the Belgian Congo.

Power

Viewed rationally, power is means rather than an end in international politics; it is a method of achieving policy objectives rather than an objective in itself. Nevertheless, the record of international relations indicates that states, particularly large and power ones, do actually view the augmentation of their power as a legitimate power objective. It may be a derived objective; that is, the increased of power may be desired in order to make possible the attainment of other goals impossible without such an increase. When the search for power takes this form, it is relatively easy to control and more apt to be brought to an end when the original objective has been reached. On the other hand, the irrational elements in such factors as nationalism may and often do provoke a state to view power as a pure objective, an end in itself.

The pursuit of power for its own sake may lead a state into extremely reckless adventures and is a major menace to peace. Statesmen whose only or principal concern is a continual search for more power should be aware of the dangerous course they are following. They may themselves be convinced of the validity of their policy, or they may be merely yielding to public pressure; in any case, they should realize that their course will meet growing resistance and, if continued to its logical conclusion, will inevitably lead to major war.

Prestige and Ideology

The twin objectives of prestige and ideology, do not permit of such translation into realistic terms, but remain abstract, absolute, and imprecise no matter how vigorously they are pursued.

Prestige: Prestige as a objective of national policy is a manifestation of extreme nationalism, and is significant contribution to the dilemma in which the world finds itself today. A state seeks to augment its prestige and avoids action that might result in a lowering of it. In general terms there can be little to quarrel within such an objective; most of us have some such tool in private lives. It is in its application to specific international situation that the trouble comes about. At times of crisis, when popular attitudes are the most inflamed, states find it increasingly difficult to adopt acceptable compromise solutions to particular disputes because of the fear that anything less than complete victory might result in a loss of 'face'.

Ideology: Ideologies serve a very useful purpose by providing norms of social behaviour and by helping to being about social stability within the state. Ideologies have certain characteristics, however, that make their function as objectives of national policy extremely troublesome. Any ideology, as it becomes widely accepted, comes to be phrased in terms of moral absolutes, as a series of self-evident propositions eternally true and immutable. These beliefs are not viewed objectively, but instead are matters of passionate conviction. Thus any dissenter from an official ideology is not only in error, but is evil as well.

When ideological differences have led to war, as in the religious wars of the sixteenth century, the wars of the French Revolution, or the nineteenth-century struggle against the Ottoman Empire, the conflicts have usually been particularly bloody and devastating. Were all the harsh words that arise out of a clash of ideologies translated into deeds, war would be perpetual. Statesmen, although realizing the unifying and propagandizing value of the ideology accepted by their people, are ever on the alert to avoid being swept away by it. A major task of a policy maker during period of crisis is to keep the temperature of his people safely below the boiling point so that their moral fervour will not express itself in ill-considered action.

Even if the war were to be won on the battlefield, the aftermath of recent wars has demonstrated that military defeat does not automatically carry with it a sense of moral turpitude in the defeated people.

Execution of Policy

In executing policy decisions, the statesman has a wide choice among techniques. The impact of international relations today extends into virtually all aspects of state life, and in appropriate circumstances almost any feature of state activity can become an effective instrument of policy. The selection of techniques that are suited to the situation and that will achieve the desired objective is one of the most important and frequently recurring tasks of the statesman. His choice among methods is governed by many factors, including considerations of time, available resources of power, and other obligations he must sustain. Although his choice among alternatives is wide, it is possible to reduce the means of execution of policy to a series of general categories.

1. ***Political Techniques***: The political technique for execution of policy is diplomacy. Diplomacy is the medium through which official contact occurs between governments, and includes the exchange of views, the communication of decisions, the discovery of disagreement, and the reaching of agreement. Through effective diplomacy it is possible for a state to bring influence to bear directly upon the decision making personnel of other governments so as to have them act in the way the state's policy dictates.

2. ***Psychological Techniques***: Psychological techniques involving the new science of mass communication are extremely effective in coping with this situation. This is most indirect method of attack upon policy, having as its object the creation of a public opinion in the other state which will force its government to act in the desired way. It operates in a variety of ways. If is often effective for a government to stir up its own people against the policy of another state and then to confront the leaders of the latter state with the phenomenon of an outraged public opinion, accompanied by a hint that unless it compiles, popular emotion will transcend restraint. This often rebounds, however, when both disputing governments have done the same thing and inflamed public feelings oppose each other.

The technique is effective if it causes the people to lose faith in their government and its leadership, and if they fall to quarreling among themselves. A government losing the confidence of its people must devote its major energy to the recapture of their trust and in this way it is weakened in the degree of resistance it can offer to outside pressure. Hitler used this device with great effectiveness before World War II. Communist propaganda since the war, although convincing very few Americans of the validity of the Soviet position, has succeeded to some extent in sowing distrust and in dividing Americans into mutually suspicious and hostile groups. The American government, aware of the lack of unanimous confidence in its integrity and in the wisdom of its policy, has been required to confine itself to steps which it knew would receive popular approval, even though great doubt might exist about their effectiveness.

3. ***Economic Techniques***: Economic techniques of policy exist in bewildering variety. This approach is also indirect, aiming to influence policy makers in other states by the application, or by the treat, of measures to weaken the national economy and to destroy the standard of living of the people. An almost limitless number of possible ways are available to bring this kind of pressure to bear. The economic interdependence of the world is such that any major interruption or diversion of the flow of international trade carries with it serious consequences.

During the League of Nations era it was widely felt that economic measures—boycott, freezing of credits, deprivation of commercial facilities—would suffice to convince any potential aggressor of the folly of its course.

The economic technique is most successful when it is used in conjunction with the others and with judicious discretion. Perhaps no other means of executing policy so causes resentment on the part of the state that is its target, and no other so invites reprisal. The current world scene of embattled economic nationalism offers proof of the facility with which economic weapons are turned back upon their users. The forms which the economic instrument can take are myriad. Import and export restrictions, the granting or withholding of international loan and grants, the manipulation of transportation and communication facilities, the freezing of credits, and even such naked pressure as the offering or withholding of food supplies are only a few examples of the economic devices statesmen are using today.

4. ***Military Techniques***: States have available to them what might be termed the physical instrumentality, that of military force. It has already become clear in our discussion that force lies at the root of any international relationship as it does in all political situations.

The socially sanctioned alternatives to force which dominate private life simply do not exist on the international plane and self-help involving violence is a much more normal event in international life than it is among private individuals.

It is therefore incumbent upon a policy maker constantly to be aware of the relative expediency of the use of the military instrument in any particular situation. It is not always necessary to engage in open combat on the battlefield in order to win an objective by military power; often it is sufficient to be willing to do so and to make that willingness known to the possible enemy.

The threat of attack by superior force, whether conveyed bluntly or subtly, will often produce the desired agreement from an opponent without the necessity of shedding blood.

In this sense it is clear that the military establishment of a state exists not so much to defeat the enemy in the field as to assist in the gaining of political objectives by the state. It may be that this interest can best be served by earning a victory over the armed forces of the enemy, but in other circumstances battlefield success might impede or even prevent the accomplishment of the state's political purpose.

The potential effectiveness of the military power of a state also has an obvious influence upon the way any government uses the only three forms of policy techniques, as well as placing upper limits upon their effectiveness.

It would be somewhat difficult for a military weak state to carry on a 'strong' diplomacy against a powerful state, since the pressure it exerted would be conditioned by its limited capacity to support it. So also with the psychological and economic instruments. No powerful state will permit propaganda harassment or economic warfare against it by a minor neighbour to continue for long if either were to become a serious annoyance.

Limiting the use of Force: One large part of the history of international relations is formed by the story of man's attempt to find a method of eliminating or limiting the use of the military instrument. States have solemnly renounced war or in general terms as 'an instrument of national policy,' and particular pairs or groups of states have agreed to the pacific settlement of disputes arising among them.

The question of war or peace in any situation is answered by the same agency that has answered it for centuries—the national states themselves. Some success has accompanied the effort to mitigate the severity of the application of the military weapon. Rules governing various aspects of warfare—the treatment of prisoners of war, the prohibition of certain weapons, the security from bombardment of 'open' and undefended cities, and the like—have been agreed upon by governments and in practice have been fairly well observed.

Growing Inexpediency of Force: Although states keep alert to employ the physical instrumentally as freely as any other, the increasing destructiveness of even a victorious war has made statesmen quite reluctant to call it into operation. The upshot of this development has been that the effectiveness of the military technique of foreign policy has been strangely reduced in recent years. It would be difficult, for example, to point to any victories gained by the United States during the period in which it enjoyed a 'monopoly' over the atomic bomb which are due only to that military advantage. Since no dispute arose during that time which made the use of such extreme measures appropriate, the opponents of the United States had no reasons to fear the bomb. So it has been with other states and the weapons. It is difficult today for policy maker to use only a little force; the technology of modern warfare is so complex that there is powerful tendency toward pushing violence to the ultimate once it has been called into play. Consequently, since no violence is practical except total violence, and since states are not easily persuaded to risk so much for any objectives except those that are truly vital, physical force is not a really ponderable factor in great power relationships today, in most circumstances.

The reckless use of power by the USA and Britain in Iraq recently gives the accounts of developed war technology and its disastrous effects on humanity.

6

Concept of National Power

There are no automatic mechanisms in international politics which guarantee to a state possession of what it ought to have or what it has a right to. States are able to gain and keep only those things which they are strong enough to acquire and retain. States differ in their capability to attain objectives; some have adequate means to work major changes in the international scene by their own efforts, while others have so little power as to be unable by themselves to bring any alternations in the course of world affairs. The closer we look at international politics the more we are impressed by the extent to which the power of states influences the objectives and policies selected by them.

Since power varies so drastically from state to state and since it plays such a critical role in determining the course of events, an appreciation of what national power is, what exactly is its role in world politics, what is composed of, and how it is measured is indispensable.

Power Concept

National power is the capacity of a state to exert coercive influence upon other states and to resist such influence exerted by other states upon it. The critical notion in the concept of power is obviously the element of coercion. When a state is able to achieve its purposes by argument, persuasion, or other means of securing free agreement from other states, such success frequently bears little relationship to the power it possesses. To qualify as a purely relationship, one of the parties involved must be forced by superior strength to act contrary to his free choice.

Therefore not all international situations are governed by power considerations. When there is identity of interest between states their relations go forward relatively free of any coercive content.

Identity of interest between states is an unusual condition, and when it occurs it is usually of short duration. Most international relationships, including all crisis situations, are motivated by the criteria of power. Normally one can expect that the state with the greatest power at its disposal will enjoy the greatest freedom of action, with the policies of the others determined by their relative rank as power entities.

Power in Politics

All political relationships are power relationships to varying extents. Political behaviour at whatever level involves the dual functions of commanding and obeying, and political science divides the members of a political community into two groups, the governors and the governed.

The problem of government at any time is that of determining appropriate commands to give to the mass of the people and then securing obedience to them. The element of physical coercion distinguishes political life from all other forms of organized social behaviour. Men are constantly being forced to subordinate their personal wishes to those who speak in the name of the state and have the power to compel obedience.

Domestic and International Power: There are certain major differences in the role of power in domestic affairs and in international politics. In civil societies there exist a number of alternatives to violence. Men have discovered that one of the outcomes of living together in groups is that they can no longer afford to govern their relations with each other purely by the verdicts of physical strength.

Accordingly a system of general rules and procedures has been adopted by each society to establish not only the rights and freedoms of individuals but also the non-violence procedures they are to follow in securing redress of their grievances.

Violence as a means of reconciling differences of opinion is reasonably far in the background in civilized societies and alternative methods are more commonly relied upon for the settlement of differences.

In international relations, owing to the lack of generally agreed-upon rules and devices to serve as a substitutes, the only ultimately efficacious means a state possesses to protect its rights and to rectify injuries is violence. The non-violent methods that exist lack both sufficient group sanction and the operating mechanisms of enforcement necessary to make them work. International politics does not go on within a super-structure of institutions so elaborate as that of domestic politics. The international community is a primitive and incomplete one with only rudimentary institutions to provide some stability.

During periods of relative calm that imperfect structure provides widely accepted non-violent procedures based upon custom; in a time of crisis there is a constant danger that it will all break down. A state is thus afforded institution protection in non-crisis situations, but it has no certain recourse except unilateral action when serious dangerous impends.

Power Channels

Political power at any level can be considered as the capacity to force individuals to behave in a prescribed manner. There are several clear channels through which power is applied to its objects. In both international and domestic politics, power may be physical, economic, or psychological, depending upon which form of pressure is utilized to secure obedience.

1. *Physical Power*: The physical channel of power involves the application or the treat of application of personal violence to individuals, either to force compliance with directives or to punish non-compliance. It may be applied to particular individuals, to groups of people, or to an entire population. It is clear that the physical is the ultimate form of coercion.

The lack of institutions and accepted alternatives to violence in international politics—alluded to earlier—illustrates the lesser role played by non-physical power in the relations of states.

2. *Economic Power*: Economic power in politics has a dual effect.

It secures obedience either by granting economic rewards or by imposing economic hardships upon its objects.

In private life economic pressures are often devastatingly effective, particularly so in modern, tightly knit, industrialized societies.

Usually economic power in international relations draws much of its strength from the physical power of the state invoking the economic weapon. States, in other words, yield to economic power of other states because it is less unpleasant to do so than to undergo the application of physical coercion. This is not to underestimate the impact of economic power, but rather once again to stress the key role of violence and force in world affairs.

3. *Psychological Power*: Psychological power in politics is fundamental in many ways. No government can long survive if every person obeys command only because of his fear of the consequences of disobedience. Government, in order to endure, requires an affirmative character; the people must obey most of the time because they want to, or in any case without even considering the possibility of disobedience. Particular attention is paid by political leaders to the problem of securing consensus from the people; usually a government is more concerned with this than it is with the application of coercive violence to disobedient individuals. This involves a liberal use of a variety of forms of psychological pressure upon the people, which can be thought of as education and propaganda.

Plato pointed out that if this task were performed to perfection no government would ever need to use violence, and laws would be useless and unnecessary. Even in as aboriginal a society as the international community, psychological power is of great importance.

As a result governments today use the psychological form of power in a broad range of ways. *Propaganda* has won some important and spectacular victories in modern times and the cold war today is marked by great propaganda efforts on both sides.

The application of psychological power has some limitations, however, in international politics. The problem of making propaganda intelligible to another people of a differing culture and value system is a very difficult one, particularly when that people are probably subject to a constant barrage of 'information' from their own government.

Public opinion in most states has closed ranks behind the respective governments and people turn a deaf ear all appeals from abroad; on the other hand, in some special instances propaganda techniques have served to separate a population from its government by undertaking popular confidence, making the government concerned less able to resist the physical power of the propagandizing state.

A good deal of the Nazi success in crushing France in 1940 stemmed from the successful German propaganda. The USA is using this technique frequently in modern times.

Power Role in International Politics

It has already been indicated that national power and the interrelations of states that have varying amounts of power at their disposal gives international politics its dominant coloration. In one form or another all international disputes tend to become power struggle and the only final settlements possible rise from the interaction of the factors of national power. Since states agree with each other only when their interests coincide or when forced to do so by superior power, it follows that any particular dispute will be resolved generally in terms of the commitments of power made by the disputing parties. All states have some power with which they back their policy, and unless one state completely crushes its opponent in a war, most disputes and in some form of compromise based upon the investment of power made by each side.

Statesmen in planning and executing a foreign policy are eternally preoccupied with questions of powers. It is of the utmost importance that a policy maker always have a realistic picture of the capabilities of his state to execute any decisions he might make. He must know his state's strength, weakness, and vulnerabilities and be aware of its military, economic and psychological position with regard to other states.

Objectives desirable in themselves are modified or abandoned entirely because of inadequate power to attain them, others are often pursued simply because under existing conditions they are easily reached.

If a system of world law governed interstate relations there would be much less need for such a preoccupation. In civil life the rights individuals enjoy are usually independent of their capacity personally to defend them, but in international politics a state is absolutely secure in its freedom only to the extent that it is capable of unilaterally guaranteeing it.

Aspects of Power

Some aspects of the concept of power are always kept in mind by statesmen engaged in its analysis and evaluation. Three of these will be considered in some detail: the relative character of power, the changing nature of power and the variable relationship between actual power and potential power. All of them illustrate the fact that national power in international affairs is not a simple and automatic regulatory mechanism, but is instead a complex and imprecise motion requiring much intense and constant application to make it beneficial.

Relativity of Power

Power is not an absolute; there is no such thing as a 'powerful' state in a vacuum. Power is the means by which a state accomplishes its objectives in dealing with other states. Therefore, a state is more or less powerful than other states, when compared with them, or it is powerful or not in terms of its ability or inability to reach its objectives. It is a common enough error to conceive of 'power' as a condition which a state seeks to achieve, but by itself the term is meaningless. Is a state as Italy powerful? Obviously one cannot give an unqualified answer.

Italy is a powerful state as far as Egypt or Peru or Thailand or Iceland is concerned, but it is a weak state from the point of view of the United States or the Russia. Consequently a state's power is meaningful only in terms of the state or states by which it is measured.

This simple fact has a profound influence upon the calculations of policy makers. They maintain a close watch upon the power situation as it affects all states, but pay particular attention to the states with which they maintain close relations and those with which they are in dispute or are likely to become so. They make a constant attempt to keep the power balance tipped in their favour as regards those particular states even though this might necessitate weakening themselves as regards other states with which their relations are less intimate.

Undercommitment and Overcommitment of Power: A further point must be made about the relativity of power. A state should apportion its power according to its objective. If a state undercommits itself and fails to support its pursuit of an objective with adequate power it will fail in its policy and all the power it did invest will be wasted.

Overcommitment often involves a state in policy steps beyond what it interest dictates and it gets entangled in the pursuit of worthless objectives or what is worse, none at all. In addition, over commitment of power usually requires the taking away of power from the support of another policy in order use it unnecessarily.

In modern international politics, where most states are committed to the practical limit, any such overcommitment means that some other policy must of necessity suffer. Not very many states today can afford to allow any policy to fall while using the power that might save it to accomplish no useful purpose in another quarter.

The Changing Power

Power is not a permanent and unchanging entity but is instead in a process of constant change. Some of the greatest policy blunders in history have come about as a result of a statesman's assumption that a given power relationship would endure indefinitely, or that factors that produced a power advantage in one situation would produce the same advantage in different circumstances. The United States, enjoying a power superiority over the USSR at the end of World War II because of the 'monopoly' of atomic weapons, implicitly assumed in its policy that this advantage would continue permanently and had no alternative procedures available to cope with a changed relationship. Soviet mastery of atomic techniques forced the American government to improvise new policies reflecting the altered power situation.

Another example of such a miscalculation of the permanence of power is furnished by the Nazi belief that blitzkreig tactics that were so effective against the West in 1940 would be equally as devastating against the Russian armies in 1941.

Pace of Change: Actually, change in power relationships is only a special instance of the relativity of the whole concept. Each state's power's in a constant process of alteration, either developing or declining. No state can stand still in terms of power.

No two states are developing in power in the same way or the same rate. As a result of this highly dynamic situation, the relations of any one state to any other being perpetually modified.

The power situation of Japan and China, for example, is not the same at this moment as it was five minutes ago. In one state or the other more babies were born, more technology mastered, more guns manufactured, more resources discovered; all of these and many other factors have a direct bearing upon the relative power relations.

Policy Safeguards against Change in Power: It is not an exaggeration to say that any power calculation in international affairs is out of date as soon as it is made. No human judgment can keep up with all the factors that affect national power, and all the information that comes to the attention of statesmen and upon which they base their judgments is outdated by the rapid march of events.

The most policy maker can do is not only to estimate the power situation at any given moment but also to attempt a projection into the future of the power status of all states involved, taking into account the trends to development as they exist. Of course, this technique ignores sudden changes in conditions which might create new situations, but an attempt is made to cope with this factor also. Insofar as possible a statesman seeks to leave open what might be called escape routes: alternative policies with adequate power support are held in reserve to be used in case sudden shifts in the situation make different tactics necessary. Irrevocable power commitments are avoided whenever possible, being entered into only under extreme compulsion or when significant change in the over-all situation is unlikely.

Finally, it may be repeated that policy decisions by a state are usually based upon providing a little more power than it is hoped will be needed, either actually committed or held in reserve. In all these ways statesmen seek to allow for the changing quality of power.

Actual and Potential Power

Another special aspect of the relativity of power is the varying relationship among the total potential of a state, is actual available power, and the proportion of its available power it is willing and able to commit in support of any particular policy. Power comparisons of states may be and often are made in terms of each of these criteria.

The measurement of power in terms of the total theoretical potential of a state is of particular value in making projections for the long-range future course of world politics and of considerable significance in estimating the possible outcome of a long and total war in which a state would be expected to muster as much of the theoretical total of its power as would be practical. The comparison of states in terms of their actual available power provides some guidance in predicting the short and middle range developments of world affairs. It also has relevant in isolating major power disparities among various states and thus in providing a means to determine probable future crisis areas.

An analysis of the power that states have available for commitment in a particular situation is the most frequent and useful form of power judgment. Regardless of theoretical potential or the available totality of power, only rarely is a state able to throw more than a portion of its power behind the support of any single policy.

It is this portion of a state's power that is involved in any particular dispute and usually controversies between states are settled in terms of partial commitments of power. Only in wars of survival do states seek to put everything they have at the service of a single policy. To say that disputes are settled generally in terms of the relative power commitments of the states involved is not to say that the more powerful state always gains its objective. Indeed, the opposite is often true, provided the lesser state is able to apply more pressure than the larger one in the given situation.

Although Britain's total power far surpassed that of Egypt, the immediate power advantage lay with Egypt and Britain ultimately withdrew its armed forces.

The Time Factor: There is obviously a time factor at work in this connection. A state may increase the power it has available for commitment in any particular dispute, or it may translate a larger proportion of its potential into power-in-being. To do either of these things, however, requires time.

To add to the power supporting any particular policy without increasing the total available power usually involves withdrawing some elements of power presently engaged in executing another policy. This normally requires many policy adjustments in several areas before it can be consummated, often a slow and painful process.

Variation from State to State: The relationship between potential power and actual power varies widely from state to state. One state may have vast potential but may be unable or unwilling to gain, or uninterested in maintaining, a high level of actual power. Such was the condition of the United States from 1920 to 1939. Others may have a much smaller potential but will keep a greater proportion of it in readiness at all times and thus cut a larger figure in world politics than a state of the first group. Pre-war Italy and Japan were both only meagrely endowed with the resources of power, but so much of what they had was in a state of permanent mobilization that they were among the giants of their day.

It is clear that there is at best a great discrepancy between the theoretical potential of a state and the practical maximum of power it can bring into being. No state can hope to realize its entire potential or even approach it; the requirements of the civilian population cannot be ignored.

In the United States, although major changes were made in the civilian way of life, the greatest total power mobilization of all time went on alongside a civilian standard of living which surpassed that of peacetime levels in most of the other parts of the world.

Factors of National Power

1. *Tangible and Intangible Factor*: The factors of power are both

tangible and intangible, and each contributes to the over-all power of a state in a manner unique for that state.

The factors are of unequal weight when applied to different states, and each interacts upon all the others. Power defies exact analysis; the most that policy makers can do is to make their judgments reflect as completely as possible reliable information and objective analysis. The factors of power involve many aspects of state life, and power comparisons are, therefore, very difficult. One state may have great resource endowment but little military strength; another may have poor resources but great industry; a third, poor industry but a highly mobilized military machine. Which is the most powerful and which is the least powerful? No general answer can be given, for power relationships among them would in practice vary depending upon the nature of any dispute and the over-all policies each state was following.

Making power comparisons, often as frustrating as comparing applies with typewriters or portraits with ball bearings, is an essential task of the practising statesman. Without it international politics could not proceed.

The discussion of the factors of power that follows is best understood if it is considered as an enumeration of the various ways in which a state is viewed when an over-all power verdict is sought. The state's situation is analyzed with regard to the impact of each of the factors, and a judgment is reached regarding the extent to which each contributes strength or weakness. The extent to which each of them modifies the others is estimated, positive and negative results are balanced, and a general and final power judgment is reached. Of course, the process is seldom carried out in its entirety for any single state; each government in the world has made such an estimate long ago to the power of every other state, and it keeps all of them in a state of constant revision as new information keeps coming to light.

No Single All-Important Power Factor: Although each of the factors of power obviously conditions the total power of the state, there have been many attempts made to argue that one or another was the single significant determinant of power relationships and the course of world affairs.

Thus, some geopoliticians argue that the geographic conditions of international politics are controlling; certain demographers see world politics as a struggle between peoples and find certain `races' bound to dominate; there is a `free material' school of international affairs which claims that resources endowments govern power and all of world politics is merely a struggle for additional reserves; most common in the assumption that national power is synonymous with military power and, thus, power relationships are determined entirely by military strength-in-being. Similar contentions have been advanced on behalf of several other power factors.

Tangible Factors of Power

The tangible factors of national power are five: geographic situation, population and manpower, natural resources, industrial and agricultural production, and military organization. Because of their more obvious and immediate relation to the concept of national power it is appropriate that we begin our analysis with the visible and concrete factors that enter into it.

Size and Shape: The state occupies a dominate portion of the earth's surface, and naturally geographic situation and configuration directly influence national power. No two states have the same geographic conditions of national life and consequently the impact of the geographic factor is different in every case. Certain geographic conditions are basic. The size of the state is of great pertinence in its power situation. In the past states of small area have become great powers, but modern requirements of defence, dispersal, and organization place the small state at a real disadvantage. The shape of the state also has power significance. Ideally the perfect state is compact, with the minimum frontier commensurate with maximum area. Irregularly shaped or discontinuous states have problems of defence and internal communication that weaken their total power. France is a good example of compactness; Chile is the arch type of the poorly shaped state, being 2600 miles long and averaging approximately 10 miles in width.

Location: Location is a geographic criterion of considerable significance. Whether a state is insular, peninsular, coastal, landlocked, or continental automatically creates conditions of advantage or disadvantage which are fundamental to all subsequent power judgments.

The insular and peninsular states naturally must give great concern to their sea defences; the landlocked state can concentrate upon land armaments. The coastal state must operate in both areas. The histories of both Great Britain and Japan have definitely been affected by their insular location; the virtually landlock situation of Russia has governed much of the policy and limited the effective power of successive governments.

Topography: Topography is another geographic fact of immediate relevance to national power. The nature of a state's frontiers, whether 'natural' (rivers, mountain ranges, or oceans) and, therefore, easy to defend, or 'artificial' and presumably very much less defensible, tends to control much of the power planning of any state. The internal formation of the land again affects power. If the interior of a state is of relatively easy access, efficient and economic means of transportation can be utilized with a consequent advantage. If the topography is broken so that a great amount of energy is required to move people and materials from place to place, to that extent the state is handicapped. The topography of the United States is generally thought to be favourable in this regard, while that of China, where mountains, deserts, valleys and rivers cut the country up into many smaller parts, is detrimental. Sometimes a broken terrain is a source of power advantage if the state is small and under constant threat of invasion.

Climate and Neighbours: Certainly extremes of weather have debilitating effect upon national power; it is quite a good deal more trouble to mobilize great amounts of power in conditions of extreme heat or extreme cold, of aridity or tropic, than in more moderate and varied climates. A final factor, only partly geographic, might be included in this list. A state's neighbours affect its power position directly. If a state is surrounded by large and more dynamic states, it is in a much less favourable position in terms of power than it would be with weak and passive neighbours.

Permanence of Geographic Factors: Generally speaking, geographic factors are the most permanent of all of those entering into a state's power position. They can change; canals and bridges can be constructed, rivers converted, mountain barriers pierced, deserts irrigated; but change in the physical conditions of a state's existence can be at most only relatively.

Developments in technology have altered many of the geographic bases of world politics. Water frontiers were formerly viewed as extremely strong; today many consider them a weakness. The sea is now more of a highway of aggression that it is a bastion. Modern transportation—land, sea, and air—make light of once formidable obstacles. As a result geographic factors in power must be constantly revised so as to take account of the changing technological picture.

Geopolitics: There are two broad schools of geopolitical thought: the sea-power point of view, which places emphasis upon the control of the waterways of its world; and the land-power of `Heartland' theory, which asserts the dominant role of certain critical land masses.

Mahan and Sea Power: The sea-power approach is usually identified with the name of Admiral Alfred Thayer Mahan of the United States, who about 1890, brilliantly expounded the thesis. He argued that owing to the greater mobility and economy of sea transportation, states that were dependent to the land, were forever doomed to inferiority to the states enjoying mass supremacy.

The Mahan theory entered into its period of eclipse once the technical problems of land transportation began to yield solutions to the combustion engine, hard surfaced highways, railways, and the airplane. Today, although naval might is yet a powerful element in world politics, the present form of the sea-power thesis has few defenders.

Mockinder and the Heartland: The `Heartland' doctrine is intimately connected with Sir Halford Mackinder, the British geographer, who was most influential after 1920. Mackinder thought of the land masses of the world as having a relationship to each other and out of this relationship grew the controlling forces of world politics.

He considered the Eurasian continent, put Africa north of the Sahara, as the heart of the world,... and termed it the 'world Island'. Here was gathered the great bulk of the manpower and resources of the globe and here everything significant in world politics took place. The remainder of the land of the world he considered as satellite islands surrounding the World Island. The Island itself be divided into two parts. The first was the centre, or 'Heartland,' which was beyond the reach of sea power, was protected by many natural barriers from the coastal areas, and which possessed human and material resources superior to those of any other region. The remainder of the World Island he called the 'Rimland'; its dominant characteristic was its division into many small states.

Within the Heartland proper there was a further geographic division of men and resources; eastern Europe was the critical area. From this breakdown he derived his famous summary of the lesson of geopolitics: `Who rules East Europe commands the Heartland; who rules the Heartland commands the World-Island; Who rules the World-Island commands the World.'

He made some later modifications in his theory in the direction of meeting these criticism. Nevertheless his evocation of the geographic fundamentals of politics has had permanent influence.

Population and Manpower Factors

International politics, like any social study, is concerned with people; quite naturally, therefore, the human resources of any state bear directly upon its national power. A state must have a minimum number of inhabitants before it can aspire to major status; the tasks of modern political life are so numerous and so varied and are performed upon such a great scale that a really small population is not able to do them. Both industrial production and manning a modern military machine requires vast numbers of people.

The exact size of the minimum necessary population to form the for a major power is, of course, indeterminate; we may gain some inkling, however, by correlating present and potential great powers with population level.

The United States, the Soviet Union, India, and China all have populations of over one hundred million, while such formerly great state as Great Britain, France and Italy are unable to play really strong role with populations in the neghbourhood of fifty of sixty million. Under conditions it would seem that the critical number lies somewhere between two figures. Power calculations involving manpower judgments process from the general assumption that the larger the population, the greater the power.

Quality of Populations: This is subject to more refined analysis, however, in terms of the quality of the population. Certain criteria are apparent: and distribution, age distribution, and general health and vigour. Clearly a population of fifty million of which thirty-five million were women, children, and aged would be less of a source of strength than one of forty million who contained eighteen million men in the military and productive age groups.

Other less obvious considerations must be taken into account. The 'efficiency' of the population in terms of education and technical training, popular habituation to the tight organization and contacts of modern society, and cohesiveness in accepting a common leadership and set of values, all bear directly upon the contribution that the population will make to the potential and actual power of the state.

Trends in Population Development: It is vital in making long-range power calculations to estimate the trends of population development. Demographic science has progressed to the point where projections of future population can be made with a reasonable degree of accuracy. These trends are constant in their effect unless upset by radical change in the condition of life in a given society, such as technological revolution, epidemic disease, birth control, or war.

When the demographic history of all states is examined with a view to determining the cycle of population development, a striking relationship appears between population and industrialization. A three-stage process seems to be common.

By these calculations the Russia and Eastern Europe generally are due for great population increase in the near future, followed later by an even more extensive increase in Asia. On the contrary the United States and Western Europe are in a relatively and absolutely unfavourable situation, with only a slight increase in prospect before the onset of stabilization. Even the last ten years, however, have provided evidence that these populations trends are not inflexible and that social patterns can and do change.

The United States birth rate, after many years of decline, reversed itself during World War II and the 'baby boom', thus, created has caused all projections of American population to be sharply revised upward. France, by a deliberate government policy, has halted the drop in the birth rate and made large families fashionable once again. These efforts are cumulative in their effects (since in increased birth rise produces larger numbers of prospective parents) and can completely increase the future prospect in the space of a single generation.

Resources

Modern national power is largely industrial power, and modern industry consists of the application of energy to raw materials. Resources of energy and raw materials are of great importance in national power and their lack proved fatal to the great power aspirations of such states as Italy and Japan.

Resources alone are not the key to power—many states with great resources endowments are not very important in world affairs—but great without guaranteed access to adequate raw materials is unthinkable. The resources of modern times are coal and iron.

Coal: Coal is the principal source of energy for industrial processes states without ample supplies are hard put to it to improvise substitute Petroleum, hydroelectric power, wood, and other energy sources occupy an important place in the hierarchy of raw materials but they cannot replace coal. There remain some formidable difficulties with which to deal, but if atomic energy should become a major source of industrial power many contemporate political judgments would have to be revised.

Iron and Steel. Iron and steel are the fundamental components of great part of modern industrial production. The age of steel demands production of many forms of steel products as the inescapable prerequisite in national power. If a state lacks either coal or iron it seeks to acquire adequate supplies by one means or another, if it lacks; if it lacks both it is likely to be doomed to inferior power status.

Following coal and iron there come a long list of raw materials of industrial production of critical significance, most of which (notably petroleum) are important because they impinge upon the coal-iron technology. Substitution for this is sometimes impossible and always difficult; however, they are seldom required in such large amounts that it is out of the question to stockpile them.

Food: Food is another class of raw material relevant to power. The extent to which a population is able to feed itself at a level sufficient to productive and military efficiency contributes to its power position. Here, it is necessary again to recognise variations between societies. A people habituated to a high standard of living will, even in time of crisis, demand more of the state's resource endowment to be devoted to civilian purpose than would a population inured to privation.

The Impact of Technological Change: It must also be added in general that the list of key raw materials changes as technological demands. A century ago petroleum was largely a waste product; today it is one of the half dozen really critical materials of the world. Magnesium is a metal whose true value is only now being realized.

We are all familiar with the global search for fissionable raw materials now going on; uranium, plutonium, and thorium are everybody words. The successful synthesization of rubber during World War II has virtually removed natural rubber from the list of critical raw materials.

Technological change may alter a state's resource position drastically, as also may the depletion of its reserves. Most mineral raw materials are implaceable; once any particular source is exhausted a new one must be found. The rate of consumption of industrial raw materials in time of war is so rapid that certain states of the world today (including the United States) face early disappearance of a large part of their proved resource endowment as an outcome of the two great world wars. When projecting power calculations into the future, statesmen must take into account the possibility of exhaustion of reserves and the time and effort necessary to being new reserves into effective utilization.

Industrial and Agricultural Production

Without raw materials a state cannot mobilize great power; the same is true of industrial production. Modern war is a struggle of machines, and a state without the means to produce the machines of war is under a major handicap.

Most often states have a problem apportioning the claims of agricultural and industry for man power and materials. Each is obliged to work out for answer in terms of its own particular international and domestic situations.

Military Organization

The most obvious and immediately available manifestation of national power is military power. Here is the visible arm of the state that is used to serve the most important policies. Much effort is made by statesmen upon the analysis of military power and power judgment i.e. often phrased in military terms. By attempting to give military strength its just place in the totality of national power, particular care must be taken to distinguish between power being and total potential.

No state remains permanently in total mobilization every government seeks to keep immediately available that portion of total military power which would protect it while it organized its potential reserve.

The sliding relationship between actuality and potentiality and the time required to go from one to the other are constant modifying factor that all military power analyses.

There are at least three major heads under which a state's military organization should be considered; size organization, and development; quality and the strategic and tactical theory governing the employment of the armed forces.

Intangible Factors of Power

There are a great many intangible factors of power; indeed, we have already seen that most of the tangible factors already examined have intangible overtones that affect their impact.

If geography, manpower, resources, industry, and military force were there was to national power, its analysis and manipulation would be but easier and more accurate. The non-specific and non-qualitative aspect of power, however, constantly intrude upon and upset any judgment based purely upon measurable phenomena; in order to make any power analysis as realistic and valid as possible it is necessary to evaluate and make due allowance for the effect of less visible but real influence.

There are countless intangible factors that impinge upon national power, we shall confine our description and analysis to four broad categories; the political, social, and economic system of a state; its level of technology and education; its national morale; and its over-all international strategic position.

Political, Economic, and Social System

Despite the propaganda of the disciples of one or another ideology, from the point of view of national power there is no political, economic, or social system that is everywhere preferable. The pattern of institutional arrangements a society affords is peculiar to itself and may be worthless for another. The only valid point of inquiry in this connection is whether the political, economic, and social system which a state has is in fact a source of strength or a source of weakness, and in what direction the society is evolving.

The Political System: As an area of power analysis, the 'political system' of a state refers to the structure and functioning of the government and its relating to the people. Whether the government is autocratic or democratic, totalitarian or limited, mild or ruthless, is in the strictest sense irrelevant.

The examination of the relation of government forms to national power may proceed upon of several bases, all of which have in common a lack of concern with whether a government is morally good or evil.

Although no political system is the best in all ways in its contribution to national power, each major contemporary type has advantages unique to itself. Dictatorships and other authoritarian governments concentrate decision making and executive power in a relatively small group and thus obtain greater speed and—presumably—efficiency of operation. The various parts of the government are kept in close relation to each other and greater co-ordination and economy of effort thus result. Democratic governments lack this advantage.

Their decision-making personnel are numerous and the relationships among them are usually more vague. Decisions often require popular ratification by the legislative branch, with probable delay and much wrangling.

Democratic government, however, grounded in a more active

consent of the people, is able to withstand stress and defeat with much more elasticity than a dictatorship. Well-established democracies are much harder to overthrow than are autocracies, and their tenacity in the face of adversity often creates strength that offsets the superior efficiency of dictatorships.

Furthermore, recent studies seem to indicate that dictatorial efficiency is not so great as had been painted; fear, suspicion, hostility, and bureaucratic inertia at the lower levels vitiate effective decision-making at the top. This was certainly the case in Nazi Germany, and a strong suspicion exists that it is true within the Soviet government.

The Economic System: By the 'economic system' of a state is meant that group of fundamental principles which govern the conditions of production and distribution. Modern economic life is complicated and there are many ways of arranging the productive process.

As in the case of the political system, a series of questions will bring out the sort of information that bears directly upon the role of the economic system in national power.

Many of the observations made about the political system are applicable in this connection also. Some state are more efficient under a vigorous system of government control of all aspects of the economy, while the United States during World War II blended government control with private initiative to produce the greatest outpouring of goods in history.

The Social System. Underlying both the political and economic systems of a state is its social system. This set of relationship has a less immediately perceptible influence upon national power than the previous two, although it occasionally emerges as the most critical factor in the power position of a state.

If the society is in a transitional period of shifting values there is more likely to be a conflict between the believers in the new order and the defenders of the old. Any such struggle, no matter how happy its eventual outcome, cannot help but represent an element of weakness in any state while it is going on. No state involved in a fundamental internal social conflict is in a position to muster very much power in support of a vigorous and expanding foreign policy.

Level of Technology and Education

A state among whose people there is a wide diffusion of technological skills is in a preferred power position. There are many tasks the effective performance of which provides sources of strength for any state. The greater the percentage of the population the government can call upon for these specialized functions the better off it is.

For this reason, the level of technology and education of a people is regarded as an important factor of power.

Literacy: Concern with the level of education begins with a consideration of such a basic fact as literacy. A population of which only a small portion is literate is difficult to organize for the purposes of national power. As modern civilization grows more complex everyone is finding it necessary to read more and write more.

Rules, directives, propaganda, and policies can be most efficiently disseminated to large numbers of people by means of the printed word. It therefore seems logical to assume that a population that cannot be so controlled because of its illiteracy represents a serious weakness in the power position of a state.

Tool Skill: As basic as literacy to national power is the distribution of tool skill throughout the people. It is trite but true to say that modern power is machine power, and a population unfamiliar and unskilled with modern machines affords a real obstacle to that state's rise to power eminence.

There is considerable evidence that a time lag exists between the introduction of modern machinery into a hitherto non-industrialized society and the enjoyment of the full advantage that such as technological change ultimately brings.

During World War II, the United States discovered that nearly any American soldier could be trained to operate complicated military machines because virtually all of them had come from backgrounds where they had been surrounded by machines and had thus gained the basic familiarity with mechanical processes. In contrast, it is reported that the Communist government of China has found that so few Chinese have any mechanical orientation whatever that a truck driver in the Chinese army is a rare specialist whose safe is jealously guarded. Machines are indeed the measure of modern powe ·, but it is sometimes forgotten that human beings operate the macl.ines.

Scientific and Technological Knowledge: Today, when so much of social life is politically pertinent this concept of the brotherhood of science is anachronistic and every state must depend for the most part upon its own efforts in the discovery of new scientific truths and technological processes. Since many of the greatest scientific discoveries and technical advances have been made as a result of the intensification of research during wartime—atomic energy is an example—every state of any stature today is making great efforts not to be left behind in the race to discover scientific principles of military and power significance.

Specialized Non-scientific Learning: The state of learning in the whole area of human knowledge other than the scientific bears upon national power. Although many of the subdivisions of knowledge are highly specialized and seemingly remote from political concerns, no one can safely predict that any information will be valueless to the state.

The United States, for example, has had to call upon the services of many specialists in out-of-the-way fields in order to meet its rapidly expanding responsibilities in foreign affairs. Strange regions, populations, and problems call for the extensive assistance of those few people who are acquainted with them in order to advise the government upon conditions and to recommend policies.

National Morale

Morale is the extent to which a people are united in a belief in the rightness of their cause, in the integrity and ability of their leaders, and in the certainty of their eventual triumph. When a people have a high degree of unity in these terms, their morale is viewed as good; if such unity is lacking their morale is poor.

Since any great mobilization of power by a state requires the active aid and support of the mass of the people, a high state of morale is indispensable if any great part of its power potential is to be made effective.

National morale is compounded of a variety of elements whose enumeration would make a list beyond the scope of this chapter. It is largely a mass emotion and is closely associated with the promptings of nationalism. Like any such popular sentiment it is subject to wide variations in response to seemingly slight stimuli.

Good and Bad Morale: Any government must make a constant effort to keep itself informed about the state of the morale of its people and to raise it if it is low to keep it high if it happens to be so.

The problem of how to handle public relations in the interest of optimum morale is a continuing problem of leadership for all statesmen. No single formula is best for all states or even for one state all the time. Any indication of popular morale may often be found in the subjects and quality of public discussion.

When public discussion ceases to confine itself to the debate of the wisdom of the moves taken in implemention of policy and begins instead to question the policy itself, the objective the policy is designed to achieve, the motives and abilities of the leadership, or the prospects of ultimate success, popular morale is at a low ebb.

Government Morale Policy: Such a state of public opinion limits the extent of popular effort in support and any policy and serves effectively to tie the government's hands. If the drop in morale is traceable to a small and discoverable group of dissentients, punitive action against these few individuals may halt the undesirable trend. If lack of information is the source of the difficulty, a deliberate policy of `taking the people into the confidence of the government' may be the remedy. Often morale is raised by making and example or a scapegoat of an unpopular official or two, or an unpopular group in the population. Most commonly, on the general principle that `nothing succeeds like success,' governments with morale problems will seek policy victories that they can present to their people as a justification of their stewardship. Diplomatic or military offensive are often undertaken for no reason other than the need or the desire to prop up sagging morale. If these measures fail and support for government programmes remains low, serious policy modifications must be considered. The government must make the recapture of mass confidence its first order of business, and its policy steps in that process must be guided by what the people demand, or at least by what they will accept. This may mean either a contraction of objectives or their expansion; in any case the statesmen concerned must do what is necessary in order to re-establish the intimate contact between themselves and the people without which morale cannot be high.

International Strategic Position

The final factor affecting the power position of a state is its strategic role and position in the world community. A state whose over-all situation, objectives, and policy are such as to minimize its dependence upon other states is therefore at an advantage; a state unable for any reason to operate extensively upon its own is for that reason weakened. The explanation for this is found in the very nature of international politics.

When they decide that any particular objective is both necessary and beyond their capacity to attain it alone, they seek allies to assist them.

When any state enters into an alliance with another, it gives up some of its freedom of action, whether in regard to its ally, toward the common object of the alliance, or toward some other aspect of international politics. This cannot help but it serve as a limiting and occasionally weakening aspect of its over-all power position.

Military Significance of Allies: The crux of the question of allies is a military consideration. A state needs allies in order to defend itself against a more powerful neighbour who might be planning an attack, or else to be in a position to make such a successful attack itself. The more conducive to war is the climate of international affairs, the more important it is for a state accurately to assess its status and make such adjustments in its international misunderstandings as seem necessary and expedient.

In the interest of forming a common front against Imperial Germany in 1902, Great Britain and Czarist Russia buried some of their most persistent points of dispute, including especially their quarrel over their rights and privileges in Persia.

Many relatively weak states have driven very hard bargains when their aid was being sought by greater powers in a time of crisis. The state which more strongly needs the assistance of allies is inevitably in a weaker position than the one which is being requested to join the common cause.

In other words, the passive state, without doing anything to merit such superiority, enjoys a significant power advantage over the state wishing the alliance. As long as the alliance endures upon its original terms this situation will continue.

Allies as a Source of Weakness: In still another way dependence upon allies often works out to be a factor of weakness. If a state must have allies in order to cope with its enemies, it can never be absolutely assured of their support even after the strongest and most binding agreements with them. States join alliances because of mutuality of interests; if the interest of any ally changes it is in logic free to shift its allegiance to the side where it feels greater advantage to itself to be found.

If it is sufficiently powerful, a state is able to compel adherence to itself by smaller associates. How effective this is depends largely upon the type of support that is needed. If the ally is valuable because of raw materials it controls or strategic territory it occupies, forced allegiance may be as efficacious as voluntary; if, however, the ally's role is one calling for large-scale military or productive effort, obligatory cooperative is usually unsatisfactory to the coercing state. Some statesmen have felt that it is better for a state to stand alone than to be plagued with a reluctant or inept ally. Very probably the Nazis had many occasions to regret the fate that threw their destinies in with Mussolini's Italy during World War II. It is a maxim of statesmanship that the power to make binding decisions must be kept in one's own hands and not conferred upon an untrustworthy ally.

7

Economic Problems

The most frequent type of international contact is economic, and the interest of individuals in this aspect of interstate relations is always high.

During the past hundred years, states have come to employ national economic power as a weapon of policy. In the process, they have materially diminished the area of economic freedom open to individuals. The trend toward increased collectivism (the growing centralization of economic control in the hands of government) which is discernible in every quarter of the world has been intensified by two very different social forces that have come to coincide in their direction. While gaining greater economic security, men have had to forego a great amount of economic freedom. Second, the requirements of international life have forced governments to exert more and more control over their domestic economies.

Economic Nationalism

The first and perhaps the most basic problem to be considered is economic nationalism. It refers to the national attitude (and the resulting policy) which assumes that the function of the national economic system is to strengthen the international hand of the state. It is thus a denial of the economic theory upon which the societies and governments of the Western world are founded.

In free societies, the primary focus of attention has continued to be the profit of individuals, even though extensive governmental intervention was permitted. In return for certain forms of protection, individuals have given up some minimal freedoms which proved to be of little worth in practice. This individualist concern with economic life had its international implications. Classical international-trade theory is a completely developed body of doctrine. In argues generally that the profit of all is best served by the creation of a world-wide free market.

Goods and services should flow across boundaries without any governmental impediment; free trade and a high velocity of exchange of goods and services are characteristics of a healthy economic order.

Mercantilism: Classical economics is largely a product of the eighteenth century and the rise of industrialism. Before that time the prevailing economic theory of international life was mercantilism. This Mercantilism differed from classical economics in that the basic economic unit was thought to be the state, rather than the individual.

The purpose of economic life was not to return private profit, but to strengthen and to enrich the state. This conferred upon the government the right to direct and control the economic life of all individuals to give the maximum benefit to the state. It was empowered to use any weapons that proved practical and effective: coercion, proscription, subsidy, and any others appropriate.

Underlying all government policy in a mercantilist regime was the idea that the state must prepare itself for the ultimate test of its power of self-preservation: war. As a result, governments sought two general economic objectives: the attainment of the highest possible degree of self-sufficiently, and the accumulation of great stores of visible wealth with which to finance a war—gold, silver, and precious stones.

The overseas empires served as markets for domestic production, as sources of raw materials, and as reservoirs of manpower. In general, therefore, mercantilism can be summarized as a rejection of the claims of the individual to economic freedom and an assertion of the superior rights and demands of the state, the 'people,' the 'community,' or some other collective abstraction.

Neo-mercantilism, or economic nationalism, rejects the antiquated economic concepts of historic mercantilism but accepts its political assumptions and much of its technique.

No longer are governments so unsophisticated as to believe that the only forms of wealth are precious metals and stones, and the simple faith in the 'favourable balance of trade' has been replaced by an understanding of the mechanism of international payments. But governments today adhere to the political rule that each state can trust no one but itself and must constantly be prepared for a forced isolation. The economic destiny of the state is all-important; it must be always ready for the necessity of conducting war, and in this process it is free to employ all the economic instruments of coercion it has available. Individual economic objectives are subordinate; private purposes that serve public goals are encouraged while others are discouraged or prohibited.

The Causes of Economic Nationalism

It must be admitted that economic internationalism, despite its theoretical defensibility, never gained anything like universal acceptance. The most frequently used device was the protective tariff, although other aspects of mercantilist practice also appeared.

Nevertheless, during most of the nineteenth century and up to World War I, commodities, services, and persons moved with remarkable freedom in international channels.

Economic Results of Two Wars: Two wars, in which immeasurable amounts of wealth were wasted and great productive facilities were destroyed, undermined the economic foundations of many states, particularly in Europe. Part of the productive plant of the major European states was wiped out and the remainder rendered obsolescent; the financial structure of most of them was also weakened by the liquidation of income sources and the exhaustion of credit.

The mechanics of international trade operated in such a way as to threaten to drain the impoverished countries of their already depleted reserves. Faced with this situation, after 1919 many European governments and several in other parts of the world undertook restrictive policies. They sought to insulate their economies from the effect of the international business cycle so as to get on with the central problem of domestic recovery with maximum speed and efficiency.

The Effect of Nationalism: The ultimate causes of economic nationalism, however, do not lie in the economic crises precipitated by war. The economic problems of the world are not confined within national boundaries but, in nearly every case, transcend them.

The issues are common to nearly all states, and the situations following World War I were such as not to be susceptible to real solution on any unilateral line.

All states attacked these problems on their own. No serious attempt at a co-operative approach to joint action was ever made between 1919 and 1939; the most ambitious undertaking, the World Economic Conference of 1933, was a failure because of the refusal of the United States to participate.

Actually, the rise of economic nationalism is best explained as a part of the rise of nationalism in general. International co-operation in the economic realm necessitates a popular recognition that all men are in the same condition and that prosperity for one group necessitates prosperity for all.

But economic tension, instead of deepening the awareness of the common plight of mankind, had just the opposite effect. In the chaos of postwar Europe after 1919, individuals were beset by a lack of both economic and social stability. The result, as we have seen, was a great wave of nationalist revival as men turned to the state for support when other loyalties proved useless and unrewarding.

It was especially insisted that the citizens of the state be freed from the competition—always characterized as 'unfair'—represented by other states. In this way the cycle was set in motion.

Economic pressures stimulated nationalism, which in turn dictated policies that served to deepen the economic imbalance. The twentieth century has witnessed the reversal of a historic trend. For three hundred years previously, men had been engaged in a 'flight from the state': a social movement that emphasized the atomistic structure of society and made the individual the focus of all social concern. The movement reached its climax in the concepts of the limited state, political democracy, and economic individualism, each developed at its fullest between 1914 and 1915.

After World War I a counter tendency asserted itself; all over the world men turned again to the state and found in political values a significance which only a few years earlier they had been denying. As a result, totalitarian government, authoritarianism, land collectivism came to replace the institutional forms of another day.

Systematic control of its international economic relationships gave a state a great advantage in dealing with other states whose citizens were free to follow their own bent. It seemed to many observers that the totalitarian governments (the first to employ these techniques extensively) had stumbled upon the real answer to the economic dilemma of the postwar world. Other governments followed their lead, but sought to make their policies just a little more extensive and rigorous than the original. The merely invited retaliation; meanwhile other states were caught up in the process.

Today no state of any consequence feels that it can trust its economic health to the mercies of the free market; each instead keeps itself in a position to take the greatest advantage possible of any lapse in the vigilance of its fellows. The fear of retaliation is perhaps the most serious impediment to the successful exploitation of the international-community sense which we have seen to exist.

Many governments are interested in making moves toward a more rational framework of economic policy, but they fear to do so because of the danger of exposing themselves to the rapacity of others. Consequently, each new step toward internationalism can be undertaken only after a tortuous course of preliminary negotiation among all parties involved and the exchange of guarantees that each will not take advantage of the other.

The Effects of Economic Nationalism

Control over Economic Life: The areas of control in which detailed regulation is common may be indicated briefly.

Regulation of production and consumption is usual. The production of commodities deemed essential to national security—such as military equipment—is encouraged or, if necessary, forced.

The manufacture of other goods is prohibited outright because of the desire to preserve stockpiles of raw materials, or some other security reason. For every control over production there is a corresponding one over consumption; goods that cannot be produced are never consumed. There are always stringent controls over international trade. Imports and exports alike fall within the scope of government action; licences and permits become a feature of international exchange.

The extent and type of control over any commodity are determined by wither of two criteria. In the first place, the commodity may have peculiar significance in itself.

Uranium ore may not be exported from the United States because of its strategic significance, while the import of textiles into the United States is limited by high tariffs because of competition with domestic production.

The second criterion arises from the political orientation of the foreign state involved. If its attitude is friendly, economic intimacy is often encouraged; if it is hostile, controls may be applied as a means of exerting pressure.

A special form of trade control is exchange regulation. If foreign currencies cannot be used to finance international exchange of goods freely, trade of necessity is reduced to a barter basis in a bilateral relationship.

This form of economic activity is always less extensive than the freer variety and is very much easier for governments to control and manipulate. A final form of economic regulation has to do with the limitations upon the international movement of persons.

Immigration may be kept low for the purpose of maintaining a high domestic wage level, as favoured by much of organized labour in the United States; it may, on the other hand, be deliberately stimulated to depress wage rates by creating labour surplus. Tourist travel may be made difficult for the people of a state while the government is inviting tourists from other lands; many European states, especially Great Britain and France, have taken this step since 1945.

Increased Political Rigidity: Striking as it does deeply into the private lives of individuals, economic nationalism serves to deepen the gulf separating national groups today.

Particularism as represented by the trend toward economic unilateralism contributes largely to the political rigidity of the world today. The cause of political separatism is particularly well served by the notion of self-sufficiency as a desirable national objective.

The old mercantilist dogma is implicit in every nationalist economic policy; the state must be willing and able to fight a war without allies in which it would be forced to depend entirely upon its own economic resources.

Objections to the economic validity of particular policies are refuted by the simple argument that 'the security of the state must be guaranteed. Thus each state pursues security through self-sufficiency.

As world boundaries are presently drawn, no state can achieve this goal. Even the United States and the USSR, each of continental expanse and both endowed more richly than any other political units, can never free themselves of dependence upon foreign sources of supply of key commodities.

Stockpiling and the discovery of synthetic substitutes are suggested as methods of escaping the necessity of foreign supply, or else expansive policies are undertaken to gain control of such sources.

As a necessary reciprocal policy, each state seeks to impede the progress of at least its principal rivals toward any kind of self-sufficiency. Thus, to the normally competitive character of international politics has been added a new and particularly resentment-provoking dimension: economic warfare.

Increased Costs to Individuals: Individual citizens bear the cost of the restrictive practices of economic nationalism. The cost of commodities purchased by the consumer is higher as a result of protective tariffs and other import controls. With the government enjoying first claim upon the output of the economy, increased costs are passed on. Critical raw materials are kept out of private production; plant renovation and new construction are dedicated to government-sponsored production; competition for labour diverts manpower from civilian employment.

The total effect of economic nationalism upon individuals may be briefly stated; it furthers either an absolute reduction in the standard of living or at least its stabilization below its optimum level. In return for this burden, the citizen receives as return the knowledge that his government is taking steps to insure itself against destructive pressure from abroad and to build up its strength against a possible war.

No one but the individual himself can decide whether these rewards are sufficient; if his decision is that the costs of economic nationalism are balanced by the return, no one else is in a position to question. He is paying an economic price for a political reward, and policies to his end will continue to be accepted and demanded as long as people feel that this is a fair exchange.

The Drift Toward Totalitarianism: Economic nationalism serves to strengthen the trend toward totalitarianism that has already placed democracy and the free society on the defensive in many parts of the world. Once government sets about regulating the daily economic activities of its citizens, no matter how genuine is its devotion to the cause of individual freedom, dangerous precedents are created. The people become accustomed to the presence of government in areas of life where formerly it was a stranger. Even though the original expansion of function was begun as the result of a crisis situation, and even though most steps are felt at first to be 'emergency' and 'temporary,' we know from experience that governments do not easily retreat from advanced areas of control.

With new authority over the lives of individuals and no necessity for justification of action other than the demands of national security, an opportunity is created for the appearance of a type of bureaucrat otherwise uncommon in democracies.

This is the man to whom political power is its own justification; he owes his ultimate loyalty not to the people servant he ostensibly is, but to some generalized abstraction: the state, the party, or the prevailing ideology. Nazi Germany and the Soviet Union are among the totalitarian states of the modern age staffed principally with this sort of personnel.

No state with a strong democratic tradition has so far completely succumbed to this type of leadership, but it is obvious that there are individual office-holders of this description in all democracies practising economic nationalism. To main the purity of democratic ideals in the face of the demands of economic nationalism demands a degree of popular and official self-discipline which is difficult to reach in a time of crisis.

International Trade Revival

Under the principles of economic nationalism, trade between states languishes everywhere in the world. Germany speaking, current practice permits only such kind and amount of trade as directly serves the political purposes of the various governments or, at best, such trade as does not interfere with concepts of national interest that are constantly expanding.

Under the impact of political considerations, trade is being forced into unnatural channels and goes forward only by generous subsidy and open coercion. The states of Eastern Europe, for example, had developed over the years a naturally complementary relationship with those in the western half of the continent, exchanging their raw materials (coal and timber) and food products for the manufactured goods and specialized services of Britain, the Low Countries, France, and Germany. The political division of Europe after 1945 brought this trade to a virtual standstill. The Iron Curtain has forced the Soviet satellites to direct their trade eastward toward Moscow. The economic facts remain that the Soviet has no deep economic need for the products of eastern Europe (except those of industrialized Czechoslovakia and East Germany) nor can the USSR provide in exchange the finished goods eastern Europe requires. The result has been a strained and mutually frustrating relationship.

In like manner, although with less a stultifying effect, the producing states of the West have suffered from the loss of their markets to the East. The only way the European democracies can pay for the imports of food and raw materials they require is by exports; denied their normal markets in Eastern Europe, they must find other outlets.

This has been a difficult task during a period when their own economies have been passing through an era of rehabilitation and transition. While it is yet visionary to conceive of a trading area which would include the whole world and in which commodities and credit would move freely, most students agree that international trade practices must be freed to some extent before there can be any lasting improvement in the world economic health.

The American Trade Problem

The trade problem facing the United States and the policy adopted for dealing with it are central to the over-all issue of the revival of international trade. The end of World War II found the United States with the greatest concentration of productive capacity ever gathered within one state.

While all the other industrial states had suffered losses in plant and reduction in capacity as a result of the war, American production had expanded greatly. From one point of view the economic situation confronting the United States bordered upon the ideal: the world was in great need of many commodities that only the United States could supply, and the industrial plant of the United States was equipped to satisfy this pent-up demand.

The course of history since 1945, however, has brought about bafflement and confusion instead of the economic Eden some had forecast. The problem of international trade has been a constant source of irritation to Americans and foreigners alike and, under a variety of disguises, has formed a part of nearly every foreign-policy venture undertaken by the United States since the war.

Continuing Elements of the Problem: Certain elements of the American trade problem are relatively permanent, arising from the political and economic structure of the world.

The first of these is the great productive capacity of the United States. Goods of all kinds are pouring out of the American industrial plant, and under a capitalist economy they must find markets.

It may indeed on occasion prove to be the margin between expression and stability; in certain industries, the percentage of exports goes much higher. Certainly it is in the American interest to export the commodities for which there is a foreign demand. The fact that an exportable surplus is always being produced makes our trade problem a continuing one.

Most of us may be familiar with the global 'dollar gap' which affects many states. The reason there is a shortage of dollars in the world arises from the wide demand for American goods which can be purchased only by dollar balances. Among the most desired commodities are industrial machinery, agricultural products, consumer goods, and energy sources (coal and petroleum). These are necessary to maintain and to raise the standard of living of peoples everywhere, as well as to create new industrial plants in underdeveloped areas.

One more factor complicating the problem is the political significance of United States exports. American policy assumes that the success of the USSR in expanding its sphere has depended largely upon economic maladjustments in many parts of the world. Although really unable to fulfil its promises, the Soviet Union has convinced millions of people that its policy favours drastic economic reform.

American goods have therefore come to be a major weapon in the struggle against Soviet Power and community ideology. United States policy assumes that a people whose demands are being satisfied under a free capitalism society would not be in a mood in listen to Soviet promises of a better world 'after the revolution.'

Impediments to Trade: Thus far in our discussion the American trade situation appears completely favourable. The goods are available for export in great quantity, the demand for them is universal, and the national interest would be served by a high level of trade.

United States Trade Policy

There has been no unanimity in American government circles on the method to be used in coping with these problems. The situation has been attacked piecemeal by policy moves essentially short-run in their outlook; at the same time, various branches of the government have pursued mutually contradictory policies. Congress seemingly remains unconvinced of the necessity of any reasoned trade policy; since 1945 each renewal of the Reciprocal Trade Agreements Act has been accompanied by bitter controversy and progressively greater limitations upon the powers of the president to take action for lower tariffs and freer trade.

The announced policy of the government, enunciated by the executive branch after the war and reiterated frequently since is to participate in all international movements for the relaxation of barriers to trade.

The Senate of the United States, however, has made clear its opposition to American participation in the International Trade Organization, and the implementation of the General Agreements on Tariffs and Trade of 1947 has gone forward without very much enthusiasm from the legislative branch.

Despite the divided counsels within the American governments, however, two general policy techniques have been developed since 1947 to increase the volume of trade.

One, the creation of purchasing power abroad, is designed to deal with the more or less short-run difficulties inherent in the post war world; the second, an attempt at a general reduction of trade barriers, looks toward a permanent enlargement of the world trading areas.

The Creation of Purchasing Power: In a number of different ways the United States government has systematically sought to eliminate or at least to reduce the effect of the lack of purchasing power abroad by the artificial creation of dollar balances.

It has been generally recognized that this can be done only for a limited time, but the policy goal has been the stimulation of foreign economies so that they would be able to continue on their own momentum after the deliberate policy of American assistance was terminated. At least four different ways were used to inject dollars in to other states.

The first-and, dollar-wise, the largest-was that of outright dollar grants to foreign governments. The principal agencies through which this programme was handled were, of course, the Economic Cooperation Administration (ECA) and its successors, the Mutual Security Administration (MSA) and the Foreign Operations Administration (FOA).

The former was confined in its effect to the sixteen 'Marshall Plan' nations that held membership in the Organization for European Economic Cooperation (OEEC); the MSA took over not only the European-grant programme in 1951 but also a congeries of other programmes in Latin America, the Middle East, and the Far East: the FOA gathered together all United States operational aid programmes in 1953. Dollar grants were direct gifts and the American Government retained sufficient control over the expenditure of the funds to see that they were expended primarily for purposes of economic reconstruction and development. This phase of the programme was substantially terminated by 1955.

The rearmament policy contributed to purchasing power abroad in several different ways: (1) the United States subsidized the rearmament of its allies directly with cash grants; (2) American construction of military installations on foreign territory and the permanent maintenance of American garrisons there directed a steady stream of dollars into the domestic economy of each host country; (3) American 'off-shore procurement' of military supplies purchased abroad represented also a considerable transfer of dollars.

The Reduction of Tariff Barriers: The United States emerged from the war officially committed to the advancement of world trade through the reduction of trade barriers and the substitution of multilateralism for bilateralism in international economics. Its principal associates in the United Nations echoed this pledge; even the USSR was on record to this effect. The vexing conditions of the postwar world, however, have served to condition and to reduce the meaning of this general policy.

Economic nationalism is at its height in most current discussion of tariff reduction. Despite this difficulty, however, the United States has participated in two general international programmes for the reduction of tariffs.

The first line of action taken by the United States was the drafting of the Charter proposed for the International Trade Organization, designed to be one of the specialized agencies of the United Nations. The organization has never come into existence, since an insufficient number of ratifications has been given.

The United States must bear a large measure of the responsibility for this inaction; the Congress has been sensitive to the various group pressures interested in the maintenance of a high level of tariff protection for American industries.

This reluctance to enter into a definite commitment was in strange contrast to the leading role of the United States in the framing of the ITO Charter in 1947.

The second major effort in the direction of the liberation of trade practices is the General Agreement on Tariffs and Trade

(GATT), entered into at Geneva in 1947 as the culmination of over one hundred sets of bilateral negotiations on tariff reduction among the twenty-three participating states.

This multilateral attempt to enact a single great tariff reduction was again made upon the invitation of the United States. Material reductions were made in tariffs as a result of the original signing of GATT.

Two later conferences were held for the same purpose: one at Annecy, France, in 1949, and the largest of all at Torquay, England, in 1950 and 1951. [Now under WTO entire scenario of trade has changed and all other trade negotiations have become futile.]

The outcome of these extensive negotiations was a disappointment to those who had hoped for major modification in the trade policies of the participants.

All states were willing to make token concessions and were eager to take advantage of any reduction in the barriers of other states. When the discussion proceeded to economic fundamentals, however, none of the states represented was willing to abandon to any real extent the pattern of trade controls under which it was presently operating.

The Free World Trade Problem

The simplest way to analyze the trade situation facing most of the non-communist states of the world is to think of its as the reciprocal of that facing the United States. Here in the United States we have the greatest supply of the world's wanted goods and are eager to sell them; we also have the bulk of the dollars which alone can pay for these commodities.

To the limited extent that it can penetrate the American market, it is handicapped by American tariff policy. These are the basic elements in the trade problem as it concerns the free world outside the United States.

Impediments to Trade: To some extent the obstacles to trade by the states of the non-communist world are the reverse of those that apply in the case of the United States.

Rearmament makes the industrial wheels of a state turn, but

it scarcely produces an exportable surplus of goods to move in international trade. Even Britain, which has made a major effort to direct its production into export channels, has found that its attempts have not eliminated its trade deficit.

Second in important among the impediments to trade are trade barriers. Trading by most free world states is handicapped by the numerous devices that stand in the way of the orderly movement of goods across international frontiers even among fellow members of the Western alliance.

In dealing with United States and in trading with each other, quotas, import and export restrictions, exchange control, subsidies, barter agreements, and the rest of the familiar techniques serve to impede the flow of trade.

Each state is able to rationalize its retention of these practices in terms of its own peculiar problems, but such rationalizations, however convincing they may be, do not move good in trade.

A final specialized impediment is currency control and the whole issue of convertibility of currencies. Although a fantastically complicated problem, we may outline it briefly. What we call 'multilateralism,' the free movement of goods from state to state in the classic fashion, requires the accumulation of credit balances by any one state in the currency of other states, and their free convertibility into any national medium of exchange.

Britain, for example, might amass a credit balance in French francs which it might wish to use to pay off a debt incurred Mexican pesos. This would require that francs be converted into pesos or either into pounds sterling according to the needs of the transaction.

For trade to flow smoothly, it is necessary that each currency of the world be freely convertible into all others in order to meet the changing requirements of credit.

In the postwar era the financial situation of many of the producing states, particularly in Europe, grew perilous. As a means of protecting the value of their own money, many states limited or prohibited the exchange of their own currency for that of other states. This was especially true when government feared the necessity of giving up their own limited dollar credits in exchange for their own money.

The reasons for exchange control of all sorts have considerable validity in light of the circumstances in which many states found themselves; we could hardly expect states to suffer bankruptcy in the name of multilateralism. what is unfortunately also true, however, is that currency control inhibits international trade.

Trade Policy in the Free World: Multilateralism desirable in theory, has been felt by most governments to be practically unattainable in their present condition. Instead, the predominant trade technique has been barter agreements and state trading upon a bilateral basis.

The OEEC and its offshoot, the European Payments Union (EPU), have been regarded as a step toward multilateralism by the states of Western Europe. In the face of dire need they have joined a common trading pool and goods have moved within Western Europe with a freedom unique in modern experience.

Observes have, however, detected the beginning of new and portentous trend: the tendency among Europeans to view the European trading area as an accomplished fact and then to plan trade relations between the new Europe and the remainder of the world on the old basis of bilateralism.

This is at best a doubtful step toward multilateralism; it is questionable if a united Europe that carries on bilateralism with the rest of the world serves in any effective way to advance the cause of revived international trade on a worldwide basis.

A final world must be side about American trade relations with the free world. Rightly or wrongly, most of the lesser states feel their economic situation to be such as to merit special consideration in trade policy from the United States.

They no longer desire cash grants; instead they ask for the opportunity to trade in American markets upon a basis of free competition. They demand that the United States open itself up in the name of multilateralism, while they (the other states) continue to enjoy the protections and advantage that bilateralism brings.

The operations of the free economy in the United States are resented, particularly its tendency toward inflation. Inflation makes the competitive position of other states unfavourable and reduces the value of their carefully husbanded dollar balances.

East-West Trade

The problem of trade between East and West, between the Soviet world and the non-communists states, is much more of a political question than an economic one. There is no economic justification for the interruption of trade between the two worlds and the constant efforts to eliminate it entirely.

The strained economic relations are a function of the bipolarity that governs so much of contemporary world politics. The decision to cut off the trade was made for the most party by United States in the hope that this would bring effective economic pressure to bear upon the Soviet Union. It is admitted that all parties are the losers in this process, but the aim of American policy is to make the USSR suffer the more; ultimately the Soviet may be obliged to come to political terms with the West in order to gain readmission to the circle of trading nations.

Strains on the Western Alliance: One aspect of the whole problem of East-West trade merits special attention. It is relatively easy for the United States to dispense with trade relations with the states behind the Iron Curtain; they were never a principal market for American industry and the economic costs which the policy entails are relatively minor compared to the possible political rewards it might win.

For the principal allies of the United States, however, and for many of the minor ones as well, to do without East-West trade involves a real sacrifice. Not only was Eastern Europe for many years a natural market for Western European industry; it assumes a special importance for European states since they fell they are being unjustly excluded from the American-controlled world market.

Consequently, the American policy of flatly forbidding its allies to trade with the Soviet world has proved to be a source of discontent and outright defiance. Britain, France, Italy the Benelux countries, all have looked longingly at the great market and the source of raw materials that lie behind the Iron Curtain.

The economic rift between the communist the non-communist worlds is only an extreme symptom of the supremacy of political considerations over all others in today's nationalistic world.

Since economic problems grow out of political and psychological conditions, it is in political and psychological terms that their solutions must be found. It is useless to search for purely economic answers.

Underdeveloped Areas and Peoples

The third economic problem area is represented by the underdeveloped areas and peoples of the world and the prospects and opportunities arising from the probability of their early opening and development. The underdeveloped areas—which in this chapter are thought to include South and Southeast Asia, the Middle East, much of Latin America, and most of Africa—have been sometimes romantically termed 'the last great frontier'.

In this enormous area live millions of people in substandard conditions of squalor, disease, or savagery. Many of the territories they inhabit, however, have great potential wealth, but nowhere is it being adequately used for the good of the inhabitant.

In the plans of the United States, Great Britain, and the United Nations to take the initiative in opening these areas to Western economic and cultural influence, there lies a possibility of adding a significant new factor to the economic structure of the world.

Economic Status of the Underdeveloped Areas: The most notable characteristic of the underdeveloped areas in an almost shocking waste, human and natural resources are employed in a recklessly inefficient manner. Labour is low in cost and is used at an extremely low level of productivity. Because labour is inefficient, the exploitation of resources—mainly agricultural and mineral—cannot be carries on at any rewarding level.

The underdeveloped areas face an unfavourable situation in international economic relations. Their low productivity prevents them from entering the world market except by the sale of raw materials and agricultural commodities. All the industrial and manufactured products that they purchase must be financed through the sale of their exports. Since they sell low-cost commodities and purchase more expensive processed ones, they are rarely able to satisfy their national demand for the goods of modern machine production. Although almost all of these areas are politically independent (most of them attained freedom fairly recently; Latin American has the longest record), they retain the marks of a 'colonial' economy.

Three different sources can be found for the urge to develop these areas. The first comes from the states of the Western world. Many of them have reached the conclusion that both their own prosperity and world economic stability would be enhanced by the creation of modern, industrialized, technologically up-to-date economies in the underdeveloped areas. By operating their own industrial plants and raising the standard of living of their peoples, they would become more attractive markets for other producing states. Increasing production in the underdeveloped parts of the world would vastly augment the supply of goods available for consumption in the world.

The peoples of the underdeveloped areas themselves are the second source of interest. The spread of national self-consciousness has helped to awaken them to an awareness of their technological backwardness; they now demand that Western technology be brought to them.

Communist expansion is the third inspiration for development. Soviet propagandists are adept at capitalizing on the social and economic inequities of the underdeveloped areas.

The Western democracies seek to undermine the Soviet appeal by proving that capitalist democracy can satisfy the legitimate demands of the people more efficiently than communism, and with less impairment of individual freedom and loss of human dignity.

The Plans of Development

Various schemes for the development of these areas are in operation at the present time; some are unilateral, some multilateral, some carried on through the United Nations.

All of them place on the people of the area the primary responsibility for initiating and carrying though any programme; the role of the outside state or agency is that of an adviser, expediter, and teacher.

Categories of Assistance: There are two main areas into which all the various types of assistance fall. The first category aims at increasing productivity and industrialization. Generally, three things are required of an underdeveloped area in order to proceed with industrialization: capital, heavy equipment, and technically trained personnel. Various devices have been worked out to permit each underdeveloped area to gain these three necessities.

Point IV: The American programme of technical cooperation and assistance to the underdeveloped areas has been known as 'Point IV' ever since it was included as the fourth foreign-policy point in President Truman's inaungural address in 1949. Although hailed at the time of its formulation as a 'bold new programme' and enthusiastically supported by its advocates in government and private life, it has never reached the proportions hoped for by many. In a period of war and crisis, the attraction of a programme of long-range scope calling for patient negotiation and constructive effort with little promise of early visible return, has never been great.

Congress approved the programme in principle, and in 1950 appropriated $ 34 million for its implementation.

In 1951 the Technical Cooperation Administration, which administered the programme, was largely absorbed into the operation of the Mutual Security Agency. This necessarily meant that the technical assistance aspect of United States aid was subordinated to military aid and rearmament.

Point IV came to be a minor adjunct to the cold-war strategy of the United States. This was a blow to many of the project's supporters, but they retained their faith and continued to press for a reaffirmation of the basic idea.

Actually, despite the budgetary and political limitations under which the programme was forced to operate, it attained considerable dimensions within a few years.

By mid-1955 agreements between the United States and over thirty states in the underdeveloped areas were in effect, providing for American technicians to furnish assistance in the development of national programmes in agriculture, education, and health—the basic areas of social rehabilitation. Programmes of industrial development were not nearly so widespread.

In the execution of the Point IV programme for the exploitation of natural resources and the development of transportation and industry, the principal stumbling block has proved to be a lack of finance capital. The original American idea had been to satisfy this requirement by means of private investment. American investors, however, have been wary; they prefer government guarantees of their loans, particularly against nationlization or expropriation of the industries they help finance. Congress has not so far been willing to make such a guarantee.

On the other hand, the underdeveloped states still retain a deep-seated and often unjustified fear of a renewed imperialism by Western states; they prefer outright grants from the United States government to private investment.

The Colombo Plan. Great Britain's major venture into the opening of underdeveloped areas is being undertaken in co-operation with the other members of the Commonwealth through the 'Colombo Plan.' This scheme for the 'Cooperative Economic Development in South and Southeast Asia' came into existence at a conference of Commonwealth Foreign Ministers at Colombo, Sri Lanka, in 1950. Its object is stated in its title; it concentrates upon Asia as the most critical area.

It originally envisaged a six-year programme of development at a total cost of about five billion dollars. Its geographic scope includes the British dominions in Asia, British colonies in the area, and such independent Southeast, Asian states as care to participate.

The programme was specifically designed to dovetail with Point IV, with United Nations programmes of technical assistance, and with any other plans that might appear in the future. Although full of promise and with a modest degrees of accomplishment, the Colombo Plan has run into some of the same difficulties as has Point. IV. The projects have proved difficult to finance. Most of the Commonwealth members are either, like Britain, already strained to the limit to finance rearmament or else are themselves short of investment capital.

There has been some tendency to look to American private investors for funds. It has been hoped that a programme in which the Commonwealth is officially participating will prove attractive enough to tempt American dollars. Thus far this approach has not been notably rewarding.

United Nations Programmes: Since its creation, the United Nations has been active programmes of economic development in the underdeveloped areas. Most of the specialized agencies have a particular interest in these regions, and the Economic and Social Council has been charged since 1948 with overall planing and supervision of United Nations activity in this field.

Many bodies were set up to carry on the work, notably the Technical Assistance Board (TAB), the Technical Assistance Committee (TAC), and the Technical Assistance Administration (TTA) within the Secretariat.

By and large, the United Nations has had the same kind of record of accomplishment and failure made by the United States and the commonwealth: expert advice is easy to provide and is welcomed by the host government, but financing the recommended projects has proved a near-impossibility.

The most obvious possible source of capital is the International Bank of Reconstruction and Development, but the Bank is following an extremely conservative course in making loans.

Most of the sizable number development projects it has finances have been self-liquidating, and we have seen that these make little contribution in themselves to long-range development.

The United Nations sends three types of technical assistance missions to host countries: survey mission, advisory missions, and operating missions. All are composed of experts, their fields of competence depending upon the requests made by the host government in the first place. By 1955, over fifty states had concluded technical-assistance agreements with the United Nations. Many of these were fellowship programmes, under the terms of which observers from underdeveloped areas travel to study technological practices in other states; there are approximately thirty genuine assistance programmes of either the survey, advisory, or operating type under way.

A wide range of functions is covered in their activities, extending from the establishment of systems of government statistics to campaigns against tropical and other diseases.

Other Plan:. The obligations of Article 73 of the United Nations Charter have brought many other development plans into being.

States responsible for non-self-governing territories have the duty of fostering not only their capacity for self-government, but also their progress toward economic and social maturity. In every case where this pledge has been taken seriously, administering authorities have set programmes in motion. In the African and Western Hemisphere portions of the British empire, in the African colonies of France, in the Belgian Congo, in the American possessions, the story is substantially the same. Responsible governments are attempting the bring the advantages of Western techniques to their subject peoples while sparing them the more unpleasant accompaniments of modern industrialization.

Reactions to the Plans

The biggest single problem is financing the ambitious projects, but a important factor in the relatively small success so far attained has been the attitude of the governments and the populations of these areas themselves.

Fear of a Renewed Imperialism: It has been noticeably present in all the negotiations between them and the various states offering assistance. Of all the southeast Asian states invited to participate in the Colombo Plan, only Burma has accepted; both Burma and Indonesia have rejected Point IV agreements with the United States. They seem unable to persuade themselves that any motive prompts the offers of assistance other than a plot to deprive them of their political freedom and control over their own economic destinies.

This helps explain why the reaction of the underdeveloped areas to the United Nations programme of assistance has been much more spontaneous and cooperative. Two reasons exist for their preference for United Nations action. In the first place, they trust the United Nations where they do not have confidence in the national States, such as Britain and the United States; second, programmes under United Nations jurisdiction remain to a considerable extent under their own control through their voting power in the General Assembly. The underdeveloped areas, if their protests are to be believed, are avid for technical assistance; rather than sacrifice their independence and freedom, however, they would seem to prefer to remain backward.

This may be an overstatement, but certainly the policy of many of the Asian states with regard to American assistance appears to bear out this view. Closely connected with the fear of imperialism is the disinclination of these states to accept political commitments along with technical assistance. This has seriously impeded American execution of aid programmes in south and southeast Asia.

The Mutual Security Act of 1951 specified that in order to receive any American assistance (including Point IV), the recipient state would be required to enter into certain commitments. These would have had the effect to joining the state to the common effort, political and military, against the forces of communism and Soviet imperialism. By and large, this has proved unacceptable to the sensitive nationalism of Asia. These states, seeking to avoid involvement in the cold war and to maintain cordial relations with both sides, considered agreement with the American conditions a surrender of their political independence.

In 1952 Myanmar rejected a MSA Pact with the United States on these grounds; the cabinet of Indonesia fell over the same issue a few weeks later. Our relations with India have been needlessly complicated because of these conditions attached to our aid.

Only Thailand, the Philippines, and Pakistan have been willing to join political support of the United States to programmes of technical assistance. The other young states of Asia insist upon the literal maintenance of their independence of status.

Resentment of Inferiority: Although realizing their need of assistance and advice, the underdeveloped areas are nevertheless resentful of their status of tutelage and resist any overt recognition of their inferiority. This often takes the form of disparaging the very Western ideas and methods they are so anxious to learn. Since technological under development is clear for all to see, the native leadership comes to place an exaggerated importance upon cultural values and political equality. Western advisers have been obliged to act with the utmost delicacy in order not to wound sensitive feelings and thus endanger the whole programme.

Resistance to Social Change: Many of the native leaders resist the social change and redistribution of economic rewards implicit in any programme of modernization, industrialization, and Westernization. Particularly in the Arab world, but generally throughout the underdeveloped areas, local leadership is drawn from an aristocratic minority.

Though sincerely patriotic and interested in the welfare of their peoples, these leaders have little relish for any programme of development that would alter the basis of political and economic power. However, was a social revolution involving the destruction of the old semifeudal structure of Iranian. This proved too much for the ruling circles in Iran. The American mission was thanked and sent home, while its proposals were laid aside. It was not until 1954, after the settlement of the Anglo-Iranian Oil Company dispute, that the first steps toward implementation of the recommendations were taken.

Summary

Some pertinent conclusions appear from the consideration of the underdeveloped areas. Politically they already form part of the world society. Economically and technologically they are still backward, but they are already indication of their unwillingness to remain so. Unable to assimilate Western processes by their own efforts, they must be furnished assistance from the outside. The attempts to give such aid have had an uneven success, owing to the hesitancy and financial inability on the part of the Western states and to a variety of forms of resistance on the part of the underdeveloped states themselves.

What is needed is the formulation and successful application of a plant that will provide the technological and financial assistance that the underdeveloped areas require and at the same time will preserve their political independence and do not irreparable injury to their dignity and sense of maturity.

The major description in this chapter is merely to depict the historical account of Economic problem areas in the international politics. With the emergence of free trade and WTO the entire scenario of world trade has changed. Major players being USA and Europe.

8

Psychological Problems in International Politics

Mahatma Gandhi has rightly said that the Nature has enough for man's need but not for his greed. At a time when individuals should be enjoying the fruits of man's progressive conquest of the physical universe, they are instead even less secure than when they were the slaves of superstition and ignorance. This is especially true in the Western world, where men are the most 'modern' in their orientation to the new technology and yet the most oppressed by individual and group fears.

Where can we find the answer to the paradox that at every turn inhibits the best efforts of statesmen to discover a better way for all humanity to follow? Man is the prisoner of his emotions. In the pursuit of the irrational and intangible ends demanded by his psyche he obstinately refuses to serve his best economic and physical interests.

The nation-state is itself a psychological phenomenon; so are the concepts of national interest, national policy, and international conflict. If that is so, then the underlying cause of all international problems can be found in the group and individual attitudes of men. No lasting change in the nature of world affairs can be accomplished without major modifications in the psychic orientation that men bring to any consideration of international matters. Only by focusing the attack upon physiological maladjustment can we bring about any change in our climate of conflict and tension.

This thought is expressed in the famous statement from the

constitution of UNESCO: 'Since was begin the minds of men, it is in the minds of men that the defences of peace must be built.'

It is relatively uncommon to approach international politics through an analysis of individual and group attitudes. Interstate relations have been studied as juristic, political, economic, military, or social phenomena, but attack upon them as psychological factors is still something new. The fields of social psychology, cultural anthropology, group dynamics, and related areas that concentrate upon group attitudes and behaviour are just beginning to make their contribution to the comprehension of world politics.

This new point of view has been of great encouragement to all who feel that the understanding and control of international politics is necessary to the future of civilization.

New insights have been developed and new hypotheses advanced. It is not our purpose here to attempt to summarize or digest the conclusions of the social psychologists and their associates.

It is sufficient to keep in mind that the psychological approach to world politics keeps us aware of the pervasive influence of psychic factors and now offers the possibility of attacking problems of interstate conflict and tension at their point of origin: the minds of men.

Ideological Conflict

Ideological conflict is not a new phenomenon in international politics. From the very beginning of the nation-state system the international political scene has furnished examples of controversies and struggles that had as their origin the existence of ideological differences.

These quarrels have demonstrated the peculiar characteristics of ideological conflict: great bitterness, long duration, and great difficulty of conclusion, whether by victory or by compromise.

The Nature of Ideologies Today

An 'ideology' is meant the more or less formalized belief system of a people: the fundamental truths which the group accepts as the basic items of its creed. Although most formal ideologies are accompanied by elaborately developed logical justifications of an almost theological character, for popular consumption they are reduced to a series of simple maxims or phrases which individuals accept as revealed truth. For example, some of the items in the American belief system are exemplified by the following familiar statements: 'all men are created equal'; 'free enterprise;' 'a government of laws and not of men' 'millions for defence but not one cent for tribute.'

All ideologies have a moral orientation. The ideology is considered to be a summary of the social virtues of the group and a mark of its unique excellence. Thus, if all men are created equal, as American believe, there is an implicit assumption that any other group which does not share the same conviction is to that extent immoral and hence of lesser worth.

Finally, if an ideology is to be truly national, there must be agreement on its terms by the overwhelming mass of the people. Many belief systems exist in any society. These are competing constantly for the loyalties of the people, and unless one triumphs over the others and succeeds in winning the adherence of the great bulk of individuals, the ideological structure of the state is incomplete.

In modern times the development of techniques of communication and propaganda has made it far easier to obtain mass agreement to the particular ideology which the ruling group in the state supports.

Major Contemporary Ideologies: The ideologies with which the world has the greatest concern today are those of the United States and the Soviet Union. The bulk of the world is caught up in the struggle between these two systems, and everyone is concerned with the eventual outcome. A brief examination of the two systems is therefore appropriate.

Soviet ideology (we are referring here to the belief system of the people as distinguished from the government) consists of a somewhat incongruous mixture of elements drawn from Russian history, Marxist theory, and Russia's indigenous European-Asiatic culture.

These interact to produce a mass attitude marked by several strong characteristic. Russian ideology stress patience, fatalism, a low regard for human belief and dignity, a fervent patriotism, a glorification of authority, a distrust of democracy, and a suspicion of everything foreign.

In the hands of the Soviet leadership these group attitudes have become very useful weapons of foreign policy and are identified in the Russian minds with the particular social system and political objectives of the Soviet government. American ideology is not so clear-cut or so easy to analyze. In the main is the traditional democratic theory of the eighteenth century, emphasizing the dignity and worth of the individual, natural law and natural rights, limited government, and the maximum freedom and self-determination of individuals and peoples.

It may almost be laid down as a historical generalization that a necessary step in the progress of a state toward maturity is the development of a distinct ideology. In all the states mentioned, governments and private groups have already spent much thought and considerable effort in working out in articulate form the fundamental beliefs which the people share and whose embodiment the policy of the government represents.

The Militancy of Contemporary Ideologies

Although ideologies are a familiar aspect of international affairs, the role they play today is more significant than it used to be because of their greater militancy.

The modern ideologies—and certainly this includes the creeds of the United States and the Soviet Union—are no longer content merely to assume the superiority of the political, economic, and social system they are demonstrate that superiority and to force its acceptance by lesser groups. The moral content of ideology today is so strong that peoples are no longer willing to enjoy their own privileged position as possessors of absolute truth, but instead cannot rest until other societies, still the prisoners of false doctrines, are shown the error of their ways and made to conform to the right.

To speak frankly, a part of the ideological equipment of major states is the demand that the area of belief of the ideology be systematically expanded. This is usually backed by a specific policy designed to accomplish that goal. Governments are therefore led into making the search for ideological conformity an essential part of their foreign policies. Such a policy is a fertile breeding ground of ideological conflict.

Soviet Ideological Policy: Perhaps it is at its most extreme form in the Soviet world, where Moscow has demanded complete ideological subjugation from as many of its satellites as it could coerce into such a relationship.

In the first years after 1945 all the states of eastern Europe were bluntly ordered by the Kremlin to make themselves over into small-scale models of the Soviet Union. Marshal Tito's expulsion from the cominform derived from his refusal to conform in every detail to directives from Moscow. It was not sufficient for these states to imitate the externals of Soviet belief and practice. What the Politburo was seeking was a genuine conversion and a revamping of the psyche of the minor states so that they would be indistinguishable from Russia.

American Ideological Policy: In the United States the official militancy of the American ideology has not assumed such extreme forms. Most of the allies of the United States have been states that already shared the basic beliefs of Americans.

American policy in Europe has tended to prefer the political leaders and parties that are identified with institutions most closely resembling their American counterparts; these have generally been of the moderate, anti-Socialist Right.

This same predisposition to identify and evaluate foreign political issues in terms of American values has shown up in American policy in Asia—with result much more unfortunate. Asiatic generally do not proceed ideologically upon the same basis as do Americans, and it is deceptive and misleading to attempt to analyze Asiatic problems in terms of such concepts as 'democracy,' 'capitalism,' or 'individualism.'

These are ideas that are real only to a vigorous middle class, and there is no middle class of any importance in Asia. Far too often for the success of American policy, what we have thought to be the 'democratic, capitalist, and individualist' elements of Asiatic society have turned out instead to be the defenders of an outworn and dying feudal authoritarianism.

The only thing these groups have had in common with

American democratic ideology was an anti-communism which in practice was more opportunistic than sincere. In Chiang Kai-Shek's China, in South Korea, in the Philippines, and in many other places, we have led ourselves astray in this manner. Whereas official American policy has not gone far in insisting on ideological conformity from the allies and associates of the United States, it must be admitted that influential private and semi-public groups in American society have vigorously advocated such militancy.

Many protests were raised when American financial assistance under the ECA was used to finance 'socialist experiments' in Britain or to perpetuate unstable political practices in France. These same groups also argue that Spain, West Germany and Greece (some include Turkey also) should receive preferred treatment among all the European allies of the United States because of the vigour of their anti-Communist policies and the unquestionably conservative and capitalist orientation of their government.

Chiang Kai-shek, Dr. Syngman Rhee, and bao Dai of Viet-Nam has been among their favourite Asian leaders for the same reasons. These groups generally represent ultra-conservative elements in American politics, whose domestic policies reflect the same preoccupation with the 'inroads of socialism' that they demonstrate in foreign affairs. Thus far they have not won the approval of the United States Government for their Programme of ideological selectivity on the basis of imitation of American institutions, but they continue to press their case.

The Totalitarian Implications of Ideologies: Modern ideologies are militant because they tend toward the totalitarian. The growth of ideological consciousness in a people is accompanied by the increasing role of the state and the augmentation of the demands made by the state upon the loyalties and services of the people.

An ideology does not become militant and totalitarian until some social force is released which destroys the prevailing belief of the mass of the people. Whenever the faith of the mass of men within a society is shaken in the fundamental truths by which they had been ordering their lives, mass insecurity grips them and they feel themselves alone and rootless in a hostile world.

For people in this condition, with their old beliefs destroyed and nothing left by which to govern their lives, a totalitarian ideology comes as a welcome relief.

If their personal inadequacies can no longer be borne, if family and church and society can no longer furnish the sense of belonging which they demand, at least as members of an ideological groups they can find a substitute that satisfies them.

Out of every great social cataclysm has come a great mass movement. In our day these take the form of national ideologies. A new example will illustrate the point. Italian Fascism, German Nazism, and Russian Bolshevism all grew out of societies that had suffered the twin shocks of internal decay and military disaster during World War I. The people of these states emerged resentful, defeated, and bitter. They flocked to the new ideologies that promised them the fulfilment they so lacked in their decadent societies; if in return the new ideologies demanded the surrender of their freedom individual choice, they reckoned the exchange of favourable one. Other examples are easy to find.

The individual is under the control of the duly chosen leadership in all his actions and responds to their commands without conscious thought. These dogmas all promise the believer a rosy personal future if he remains true to the faith and performs his duties diligently.

Ideological Conflict in International Politics

In a very real sense ideological conflict represents the clash of masses of people rather than of governments, and it tends to take place in an atmosphere of profound popular emotional involvement.

To the extent that ideological issues are involved in interstate disputes, they aggravate the severity of any disagreement and serve to intensify and perpetuate the struggle. Resolution of the conflict becomes extremely difficult unless the ideological quarrel is either settled, ignored, or allowed to die away naturally. Much of the rigidity of the present political structure of the world is caused by the extent to which mass emotions are involved on both sides of every dispute, and the best efforts of statesmen to reduce the tension are often frustrated by the very stubbornness of the ideological orientation which in one way or another they helped to create.

Salient Features of Ideological Conflict

1. *Moralistic Orientation*: Ideological conflict is a struggle of differing moral codes. All ideologies are summations of the principles of moral right and wrong by which a society governs its conduct, and in any ideological clash there is bound to be disagreement on certain of these principles.

When moral issues are involved, the defenders of each ideological position inescapably tend to identify themselves with truth, virtue, and right; their opponents become the antithesis of each of these. Ideological adversaries view their opponents as being guilty of far more than mere error; their offense is greater because of the moral issue involved.

Any group, internal or foreign, which disagrees with the prevailing creed is by that fact sinful and evil; the opponent is an enemy of everything that the group stands for.

This makes ideological warfare between states a peculiarly bitter relationship, since each participant considers its enemy to be the embodiment of evil and as endangering the fundamental principles of society. In such an atmosphere it becomes very difficult for any issue of the dispute to be considered on its merits, since each is viewed in the peculiar light thrown by the intense ideological struggle.

The fact that 'trust' has little to do with the establishment of any working relationship between two great powers is simply ignored because of our ideological predisposition. The Soviets have reacted in the same way.

Persistence: On moral issues there is no ground for satisfactory compromise; as a result, ideological quarrels are persistent and difficult to dispose of that the eventual triumph of the good is inevitable. It is, therefore, unnecessary, in addition to being immoral in itself, to seek to compromise with evil as a way of ending a dispute.

As a result, an ideological quarrel between states drags on and on, since neither side can find any moral justification for ending it short of total victory. Indeed, no basis short of complete triumph can usually be found that would be acceptable to all parties.

The cold war provides a good example of this tendency. From

the American point of view, the danger that must be avoided at all costs in Russo-American relations is 'appeasement.' Which is meant any American concession that might represent some partial agreement with the Soviet ideological position.

'Appeasement' as a concept grew out of the pre-1939 period when the diplomats of Western Europe sought to satiate Hitler by allowing him to make one territorial seizure after another. The failure of this policy made a deep impression on the American consciousness, and its rejection is a basic tenet in the American ideological position today. In order to avoid the temptations of appeasement, American attitudes stress the ideological depravity of the Soviet and ruthlessly dismiss any possibility of a compromise between the USSR and the United States as 'wishful thinking.'

Therefore, on any agreement with the Soviet Union American policy places prerequisites that would have the effect of gaining the essential ideological point for which the United States is contending; by and large they add up to a confession by the Soviet that everything it has done since 1945 has been morally wrong.

No doubt, no Soviet diplomat will agree to any such moral judgment on the conduct of his own state: indeed, Soviet ideology demand as such from the United States in return.

Inconclusiveness: It is almost impossible to win an ideological battle in any ordinary sense. Since moral issues are so deeply involved, the only way in which one party can gain any meaningful victory is for its opponent to admit that it was in the wrong. Furthermore, to be truly satisfying, this admission must not be the result of coercion or an unwilling concession, but must represent a sincere change of heart and a genuine sense of repentance.

It is difficult to imagine any set of circumstances that would induce a people to renounce their ideology and to accept instead the creed of another state; particularly is this true in a period when the people concerned have been busy defending their own system and reinforcing their loyalties against what they have felt to be hostile onslaughts.

To expect a people enthusiastically to endorse a judgment of moral turpitude against themselves is to expect a great deal, yet this is what each party to an ideological conflict is seeking.

Defeat in World War II did nothing to alter the fundamental beliefs of the German of Japanese people; the Allies recognized this when they undertook the reconstruction of the society and the re-education of the people of these states. A military defeat induces the defeated people to reflect upon the causes of their setback and to resolve to do bettle next time; it seldom, if ever, causes them to feel that they were sinful, immoral, or wrong in the policies they undertook to support by the war.

Ideological War: There is no doubt that ideological war—that is, war fought only for ideological objectives—would be the most frightful kind of struggle imaginable.

If such a war involved the two great political blocs of the world, one of two outcomes would be inevitable: the utter extermination of one of the camps, or the mutual exhaustion of both of them. In either case the destruction and loss of life might mean the collapse of modern civilization.

Any ideological war today would be fought with a bitterness and a tenacity that would permit of no other result because of the fundamental character of the emotional issues involved.

Of all the possible bases for armed conflict between the Soviet and the Western blocs, however, ideological differences would appear to be one of the least likely.

The leaders in both great camps realize the danger of any such ideological conflict and they are always careful not to permit themselves to be pushed too far.

War in modern world politics is a desperate gamble at best; realistic leadership preserves the use of war for situations offering substantial gain and sufficient promise of success to justify extreme measures.

The gain to be derived from any ideological war is insubstantial at best and probably would prove illusory, and the prospects of victory are so clouded under the present distribution of power as to make any adventure of this kind foolhardy. War is always possible in international politics, and ideological war is always a danger; if global war comes to this generation, however, it will in all probability arise out of a clash of interest in concrete situations rather than through antipathies grounded in ideological issues.

The Falsity of Ideological Issues: Ideological issue are false, and ideological conflict is pointless and futile because of one simple fact: international politics does not consist of a quarrel between absolute good and absolute evil. It consists, instead, of human pursuing realistic objectives in the material world.

World politics is by its very nature relative, not absolute. An ideological policy that phrases an issue in absolute moral terms and pursues it by absolute means in search of absolute victory is a policy that can never attain success in the real world. It serves only to confuse and complicate a situation that by its very nature is already sufficiently complex.

Thus a government that devotes any considerable portion of its policy and power to the pursuit of ideological goals is to that extent diluting and weakening its concentration on what should be its primary business, the prosecution of its national interest.

Why did the ideological quarrel develop? The initial cause is, of course, the ideological gulf that exists between the two states, and certainly without this fundamental cleavage the quarrel would not have grown to its present proportions. But ideological divergencies exist between many other states without the development of such bitter controversy. It is noteworthy that the ideological differences existed between the United States and the Soviet Union before 1945, long before the cold war began or was even dreamed of.

During and after World War II the two states were thrown into a close, almost intimate relationship with each other for which both were unprepared. Neither had any familiarity with the other; no bond of common experience or sympathy derived from long contact provided a common ground.

The differences between the two cultures, the social and political organizations, and the belief systems burst upon the two peoples with great suddenness. Neither side made any great effort to understand the other; indeed, circumstances were such that any such effort would have been very difficult of accomplishment even if the will had been present.

The ideologies of both states were inherently expansionist. Both Marxist communism and individualistic democracy implicitly assume the eventual conquest of all men by their doctrines; both look forward to the rapid expansion of their areas of acceptance.

This idea was at first imperfectly understood by both states, and each saw no necessary conflict between the two theories, during the war there was much discussion in both states about the extent of ideological unit that existed, but closer examination revealed the basic dynamism of both democracy and communism.

The expansion each ideology required affected all postwar relationships between the two states and contributed in large measure to the ideological controversy of today.

Ideological Issues: No complete listing of the ideological issues between the two states is possible without making a detailed point-by-point analysis of the two creeds. In general, however, it can be said that the quarrel centres around three great points, each of which represents a whole family of specific issues.

The first of these is the world role to be played by the two states. Each ideology looks forward to the day when the world is organized entirely in harmony with its principles; each assumes that its states is destined to be the one true world leader.

This leads to constant policy disagreements between them as each seeks to realize its own destiny and to impede the progress of the other. Ideologically there is no room for peaceful co-existence, let alone harmony and cooperation; each ideology assumes the necessity for victory over the other.

Thus, ideology makes the Soviet Union and the United States natural and eternal enemies, since both aspire to a position of leadership that can be occupied by only one.

Whether the Soviet Union is good or evil, moral or immoral, is in the strictest sense immaterial to the United States; what should concern our government entirely is the real threat posed to American national interest everywhere in the world by the Soviet government and Russian power.

Russian-American Ideological Conflict

Some special attention must be paid to the Russian-American ideological conflict in the light of the characteristics of such disputes just discussed. There is no doubt that this is the greatest such quarrel in the modern world and perhaps the greatest of all time; certainly its potentialities for destruction far surpass any others afforded by history. An understanding of some of the features of the conflict is necessary to a comprehension of the basic forces of world affairs.

Reasons of Russian-American Ideological Conflict

To Americans, Russian power, Soviet-style government, and communism are all the acme of immorality and sin, while American power, political democracy and capitalism are highly moral and good.

As one would expect, Soviet expositions of the same points take exactly the opposite tack.

The Future of the Ideological Conflict: The generalizations about the termination of ideological conflict apply with particular emphasis to the Soviet-American dispute. The controversy has been going on since the end of World War II and shows no signs of abating; indeed, the differences are deepening and appear to be permanent. Up to the present time no suggested compromise on the ideological issues has stood the slightest chance of acceptance. No one can now be certain of the future course of the struggle, but it will be very probably result eventually in one of three possible outcomes.

The first possibility is that the conflict will intensify to the point of ideological war.

The second is permanent continuation of the struggle until it becomes an accepted way of life; Orwell's vision of the world in 1984 assumed this outcome.

The perpetuation of the ideological conflict would also nullify any attempts at the removal of the real objects of controversy between the states by the diplomatic techniques of compromise; no improvement in political relations would be possible.

One more outcome of the ideological struggle is its gradual relaxation until it either disappears or else diminishes to the point where at permits more or less normal relationships between the governments on policy matters. This is the happiest possible outcome, for if it took place a real improvement in the climate of world affairs would occur.

Other ideological quarrels of the past have ultimately been put aside by their participants: Britain and France, Britain and the United States, and Greece and Turkey are examples of former ideological foes who were able to discover enough in common to make closer relationships possible on a basis of identity of interest.

Other Ideological Conflicts

Although the Soviet-American ideological conflict is the greatest and most significant one in the world today, it is far from being the only one. Such quarrels can be found in many other parts of the world, differing from the massive dispute between the two giants only in specific issues.

The European-American Dispute: Born of the frictions arising from the very closeness of the western alliance against the Soviet Union, the American-European ideological struggle is a relative newcomer to the family of such quarrels and is still peripheral in its impact.

The bloc included in the NATO has a great deal in common with the United States including agreement on most fundamentals of belief. Nevertheless, the tensions of the postwar world and the requirements of policy have produced considerable ideological disagreement and this threatens to become worse if the bipolar world dissolves.

Europeans condemn American immaturity, materialism, impatience, and preoccupation with physical power. They also find much fault with American culture and delight in making many invidious comparisons with themselves. Americans, on the other hand, point out European decadence, impracticality, and over-sophistication as contrasting with the simpler but more wholesome American way of life.

Americans criticize European inability to understand or to employ the techniques of political democracy; Europeans point to political corruption in the United States and inconsistencies in policy and inquire if American democracy is after all so much more successful than the European variety. All in all, the dispute between Europe and the United States is at the present time more of an annoyance than a danger to orderly relationships.

Asiatic-Western Conflict. By the same token, serious ideological difference exist between the international communist movement and this same Asiatic ideological pattern. Although Soviet policy has been more successful than American in coping with 'the new Asia.' This success has been more through Soviet adoption of Asiatic nationalist goals than through the inculcation of ideological harmony. Actually, whenever the Soviet has attempted to disseminate the pure Moscow ideological line it has met instant and concerted resistance.

Nowhere in Asia is communism a true mass movement. Even in China the communist ideology is the possession of only a small elite group of Chinese who feel themselves uprooted from their heritage and this have become susceptible to the Marxist line.

Despite the superficial identity in belief which is displayed by Moscow and Peking, Mao Tse-Tung himself is the authority for the statement that the goal of the present regime in China is to 'signifiy' Marxism so as to make it palatable to the local conditions.

Communism has failed to strike deep roots into the soil of Asia for the same reasons as has Western democracy. Individualism simply does not have any meaning for Asians; their society is geared to group life—the family, the tribe, the clan—and the individual gains significance only as a member of a larger community.

We turn now to a brief examination of the more extreme forms of nationalism as they occur in the world today. Throughout our discussion of world politics the phenomenon of nationalism has been constantly in the foreground.

Nationalism Status Today

The emotion of nationalism is undergoing a multi-formed development, both in direction and in speed, in various parts of the world. In some areas nationalist loyalties are losing their effectiveness and are being replaced by a growing allegiance to a larger basis of organization than the state.

In others, however, the decline of nationalism has not been followed by the appearance of a new loyalty and a vacuum of belief has thus been created. At the same time other parts of the world are still in the expanding stage of nationalism; the old appeals retain their potency and indeed their effectiveness may be increasing. It is in these last-named areas that there develops what we call the 'cult of nationalism.'

Areas of Declining Nationalism: Although a decline in the degree and extent of nationalist commitment by individuals has taken place in many states during the past two decades, in Western Europe this condition has become so widespread as to attain the status of something like a mass movement.

Individual identification with nationalist goals has sharply decreased in such states as Italy, France, the Low Countries, Scandinavia (notably Denmark and Norway), and West Germany. Many reasons have been advanced to explain this development, and several unquestionably have some pertinence.

Among these are the disillusionment brought about the two wars in one generation diminish importance placed upon 'political' values; the cyclical course often taken by nationalism; and the recognition of the inefficiency of the nation-state, at least on a scale as small as that found in Western Europe.

In any case, nationalist attitudes have decreased in potency to such an extent that proposals for lasting European Union or consolidation are farther advance in the middle of the twentieth century than they have been at any time since the days of Charlemagne.

The principal new vehicle of popular loyalty is the growing idea of a European community, although there is considerable sentiment favouring the world-wide organization of political society. On the other side of the world, another state showing signs of being in the declining stage of nationalism is Japan; the same factors are work here.

It may be that the cyclical theory of nationalism will be proved wrong and that these and all the other states now dismantling their nationalist apparatus will ultimately return to their former ways. On balance, however, the indications still point to the continued progress of all them toward some new and perhaps broader basis of loyalty.

Areas of Expanding Nationalism: In opposition to the foregoing trend, however, many other peoples are still in the growing and expanding stage of nationalism. These states are of two types: the newly great large states, including the United States and the Soviet Union in one group and China and India in another, and the smaller states, including both those that have only recently become independent and those whose popular consciousness is newly formed despite a longer period of legal independence. Among the smaller states whose nationalism is most extreme are the Argentine and Brazil in the western hemisphere; Ireland, Poland, and Yugoslavia in Europe; Egypt and the Union of South Africa in Africa; Iran, and Turkey in Southwest Asia; Indonesia, Myanmar, and the Philippines in Southeast Asia; and Korea in the Far East.

Salient Features of the Cult of Nationalism

In many of the states in which nationalist attitudes are on the rise, there exists a condition that may be termed 'pathological' nationalism or the 'cult of nationalism.' This arises when the intensity of nationalist feelings rises to the point where the normal set of social values is drastically altered and national goals and aims are elevated to a position of unchallenged superiority over all others. Not only does individual loyalty to other groupings, such as family, trade union, church, temple and so on, diminish sharply, but in many cases the private person is denied the right to membership in these groups if their demands conflict with those of the state. Pathological nationalism has an immediate and marked effect on the conduct of foreign affairs by the government, and often forces a policy entirely different from the one that would be if nationalist demands were kept at a more restrained level.

Totalitarianism: In the first pace, extremist nationalism is totalitarian: that is, it encompasses every aspect of individual behaviour. Every moment of the day the individual is reminded that he is a part of the greater whole, the nation, and in all his actions he is charged with a responsibility to it. His economic life, his family life, his religious life, his recreational life, all of these are functions of his fundamental and most important level of being as a member of a national group. The individual cannot escape the nation. The criterion of 'patriotism' or loyalty' or 'good citizenship' is applied to everything he does, no matter how personal or intimate. In fascist Italy, for example, it was regarded as a mark of good citizenship to many early and to have large families; such a course was urged upon Italians as a means of showing their patriotism. Nazi Germany went farther: such was the demand for children that unmarried German girls were feted to produce them (especially boys).

Authoritarianism: The cult of nationalism is also authoritarian. The political values of nationalism intrude into all areas of the individual's life; the longer state becomes a supreme arbiter of all modes of human conduct. Men are no longer permitted freedom of choice in situation in which formerly the state had no legitimate interest; every choice, being fraught with political significance, become a legitimate matter of state concern and direction. In free societies, the line of employment a man follows is felt to individual discretion and circumstances; a super-nationalist nation comes more and more to place men in the position in which they will contribute most directly to the national strength.

Both Nazi Germany and Soviet Russia have forced individuals into particular jobs, decreed where they should live, destroyed 'unpatriotic' organizations and substituted new ones in which private membership was obligatory, and even sought to undermine the family institution as a dangerous rival of the state for the loyalty of the people.

Authoritarianism and totalitarianism are really two aspects of the same phenomenon: the popular rejection of individual freedom, in return, for the great psychic security obtained from membership and participation in the great entity of the nation.

A rough but reasonably accurate guide to the degree to which any particular nationalism has reached the proportions of a cult is the determination of the extent to which they have transferred the control over the many intimate details of private life to the national and to its external manifestation, the state.

Emotionalism: The new nationalism, representing as it does a great emotional commitment on the part of the people, is extremely sensitive and unstable Nationalist outburst with profound policy coursequences are likely to occur at anytime in a people whose sense of political identification with their government and with each other is deep and immediate. A sense of 'national honour' is keen and the people are ever alert to discover and slight on it by any other group, to resent it keenly and to demand that their government obtain immediate satisfaction.

Impatience: A final characteristic of the cult of nationalism has a special pertinence in a crisis situation involving international conflict. Being so charged with emotionalism, highly nationalist people tend to be extremely impatient.

Nothing is more frustrating to an individual than to undergo a strong emotional experience preparatory to action, and, then, to have that action indefinitely postponed. In such a situation there is a tendency toward an explosion of some sort simply as a way of relief from a tension that has grown unbearable.

Great Powers and Extreme Nationalism

In the great powers today there is a clear tendency toward the type of nationalism we have been discussing. In the United States and in the Soviet Union, in China and in India, nationalist attitudes all point in the same direction, although to different extents.

The most advanced forms are found, of course, in the Soviet Union and in China; the United States and India have not yet reached the same pitch.

In the USSR a frankly totalitarian and authoritarian nationalist creed subordinates all individual life to the constant demands of the state. Nazi Germany is the only modern rival to the USSR in the degree and extent of control exercised over the individual in the name of the international mission of the state.

In China, the undeveloped nature of the Chinese economy and society has made the task of creating a belligerent Chinese nationalism more difficult for the communist rulers, but their objectives are clear, and much progress has already been made.

In the United States, the traditions of individual freedom have stood in the way of any rapid movement toward anything like Nazi or Soviet nationalism. Nevertheless, the concept of 'national duty' generally accepted by Americans today is much broader than it was twenty years ago; the responsibilities of nationalism bear much more heavily now.

The demand for conformity, the discouragement of dissent, and the rise of anti-intellectualism are only three indices of the extent of the growth American nationalism.

Indian nationalism is still formative; however, the struggle for independence from Britain gave the mass of the population the beginnings of a real nationalist spirit. Events since independence have served to conform and strengthen this tendency.

Characteristics: Large-state nationalism has a few characteristics that mark it off from the small-power variety. Most noticeable is a drive towards leadership. Of the four states mentioned above, two—the United States and the USSR—are accepted as great powers, while China and India aspire to that status.

American nationalism dreams of a world organized according to an American plan in which happiness would be universal under our leadership; the USSR frankly admits its goal of a communist world.

India has not yet raised its sights higher than Asian leadership and acceptance as an equal at the council tables of the world.

The problem has been most frustrating for China. Being a revolutionary government, and a communist one as well, the new regime has been treated as a pariah by the United States and many of its allies.

Diplomatic recognition and admission into the United Nations were sought frantically by the Chinese communists as being formal evidence of their arrival at international respectability and world leadership. The longer these were denied and more insistent Chinese nationalism became in demanding them.

A second nationalist characteristic is expansionism. Nationalism demands that great states export and impose their ideology upon their lesser neighbours. This is sometimes called 'cultural imperialism'—a deliberate policy of forcing a major power's cultural standards on such states that are unable to resist successfully.

It is usually a matter of great gratification when a small state adopts some particular cultural practice of a large one. Americans are generally quite pleased that Coca-Cola has become popular in Europe and Asia

A large state that is highly nationalistic is convinced of the innate superiority and rectitude of its institutions and its policy.

Therefore, in any international situation touched up by the nationalist credo, it is impossible for such a state to adopt any attitude but that of attempted dictation. Free discussion between equals is impossible because in terms of the nationalist attitudes the participants are not at all equal; one state is right and the other wrong.

Small States and the Cult of Nationalism

As named earlier some of the smaller powers of the world whose policy indicates that they are in the grip of virulent nationalism. We found them to be located in nearly every part of the world: the Western hemisphere, Europe, Africa, southwest Asia, southeast Asia, and the Far East. East of these states faces unique circumstances and is in a different stage of national development.

As a result, each has demonstrated its nationalist orientation in a fashion peculiar to itself. Nevertheless, it is possible to distinguish in their behaviour certain common characteristics which we might list as marking off small-state nationalism.

Defensive Orientation: In the first place small-state nationalism is different in that it is primarily defensive. The nationalist attitudes of the great powers are affirmative and positive in direction; these peoples look forward to ever increasing power, glory, and importance. On the other hand, the fundamental nationalist point of view of the people of a minor power is negative; nationalist emotions are directed against something or somebody.

All of them are determined never to slip back into the condition from which they are emerging, and all the resources of nationalist persuasion are devoted to keeping the people alert to the danger of doing so.

Introversion and Xenophobia: The consciousness of their bitter past and the stimulation of nationalist sentiments has turned nearly all the peoples of the small states inward in their search for social values. In every state mentioned the cultural history of the people has been repeatedly searched to discover ancient traditions and virtues which are applicable to their present status of independence.

The rejection of everything alien, even if it is good, is demanded by the more extreme advocates of a purely indigenous nationalism. This lends it a strangely withdrawn character. Whereas large states are seeking to extend the scope of their nationalist creed, the small states reverse the direction and attempts to confine their doctrine to the minimum group of people who share the common tradition.

In the Muslim world—including Iran, Egypt, Indonesia, and Pakistan—extremist nationalism is allied with Muslim fanaticism, and the most vociferous spokesmen for the destruction of foreign influence and the retreat into obscurantist primitivism are religious leaders.

In Israel, the same tendency can be seen: the strictly Orthodox Hebrew leader are insistent upon the minimum contact with the outside world. In the western Hemisphere, each of the various Latin American states is seeking out its Spanish (of Portuguese) heritage. Ireland's insistence on the deliberate recreation of its Gaelic culture is another example of this introversion.

Belligerent Independence: We have already remarked on the belligerent independence of smaller states whose nationalism is aroused. This reaction is not a surprising one, for it is derived from history and the course of world politics.

The government of Indonesia learned this to its sorrow. In 1952 a cabinet fell from power because it had negotiated a mutual-security agreement with the United States and made overly great concessions to American policy.

Accommodation of Cultures

It is the pattern of emotional reactions produced in people of all states when they are brought into sudden and intimate contact with cultures other than their own.

In one sense it is obvious that the creation of a world political system that will bring peace and security instead of perpetuating crisis must depend on first bringing into existence a widely based sense of a common destiny among men everywhere. Chapter 9 was devoted to a consideration of the extent to which an international-community sense has developed.

Political harmony among states must wait upon the construction of a shared system of values which men in all parts of the world accept and act upon.

Most of these values are what sociologists call 'culture,' and the present disharmony, which is reflected in nationalist disagreements and international political conflict, is rooted essentially in cultural tensions. The accommodation of cultures is certainly as important as any other single problem in international relations, and may perhaps be the most critical.

Intercultural Contact and Tension

The Role of Technology: Intercultural contacts between peoples have been greatly accelerated in the last century by the impact of technology. Societies formerly were permitted to isolate themselves and to develop their own value system and institutions in terms of their own evolution.

Many of these contacts have been sudden and forcible; one example among many is the dramatic 'opening' of Japan to the outside world by commodore Perry of the United States in 1854. Today, with political organization on a world-wide scale a reality in the United Nations and with the great powers and many lesser ones carrying foreign policies which project their interest and their power into the out-of-the-way places of the world, the comfortable cultural isolation which most societies enjoyed not too many years ago is a thing of the past.

Intercultural Tension: Close and frequent intercultural contacts between widely differing groups inevitably produce many possible points of friction. Once international relations break through the barrier of formal interstate contact and become a matter of 'peoples speaking to peoples'—and technology makes this increasingly the case—the possibilities for misunderstanding, lack of sympathy, disagreement, and conflict multiply as the many cultural differences are discovered and seized upon.

Areas of Intercultural Tension: Any of the myriad social relations that go to make up a culture may serve as an area of intercultural tension; there is no way to predict in advance which particular social custom will produce such tension.

Nevertheless, certain broad areas are common sources. The first area is that of moral codes. Standards of good and evil differ and disagreement in these terms is likely to be fundamental and acrimonious.

Perhaps, a protection of the moral issue is the conflict that arises over different systems of personal and family life, particularly, codes of sexual behaviour. Also in this category is the issue of religious belief and organization, particularly, involving evangelical, missionary faiths.

Accustomed to thinking Asians as pagans who had not been shown the true reason, Americans today sometimes find it difficult to take these people seriously in political terms.

Another area of intercultural tension is intellectual life. This arises today largely because of the western assumption that Oriental societies have no intellectual tradition worthy of consideration. Stemming from unquestioned western superiority in technology and science, this attitude has been extended into the humanistic fields. Asiatic resentment at being considered the intellectual inferior of the West is natural. A final area of tension is that political, economic, and social organization. These institutional structures are always an outgrowth of the particular tradition and value system of a people, and quarrels about the superiority of one over another can never be decided in any rational way.

Political Results: Probably the most immediate political effect of an interculture disagreement is the immediate stimulation of the nationalist attitudes of the people involved. Faced with a strange and often disquieting lack of understanding from another people, each group turns for reassurance to its own creed and draws strength from the reaffirmation of its principles.

The Briton who journeys abroad and punctuates his trip with repeated rejections of everything foreign is a stock character. Thus, intercultural disharmony serves to deepen and strengthen the other divisive factors at work in international politics.

The effects of this division on the actual policies of governments have already been noted: an increasing rigidity in the relations of the states involved and the consequent difficulty of settling disputes as they arise. It is this fact which has led some observes to suggest that the best course for the United States to follow in its relations with the USSR is to have as little to do with it as possible. In that way intercultural contacts would be minimized, fewer points of nationalist conflict would arise, and the possibility of amicable adjusting the conflicts interest that do come up would be greatly strengthened.

Effects on the United States and India

The problem of inter-cultural tension and of the need of inter-cultural understanding is particularly pressing as it affects the United States and India. This is true for a double reason. In the first place American policy has as its ultimate goal the creation of a world community of tightly knit relationships governed by world law.

We have seen that such a society is possible only on the basis of a high degree of cultural integration or accommodation. Secondly, the problems of intercultural adjustment have been more perplexing for Americans than for any other people of the Western world since 1945. For no one else has it been so important to develop techniques for intercultural adjustment, and for no other people has the task been so difficult.

The Nature of American Culture: Of the many things that can be said about the broad subject of American culture, only a few are especially pertinent to the present discussion. Perhaps the most significant aspect of the American cultural pattern is that it is highly indigenous. Although originally an offshoot of the main stem of the Western tradition, American environmental factors speedily altered the direction and speed of development until a distinctly American way of life appeared.

Throughout its entire formative period the American consciousness was generally turned inward in search of the peculiar manifestations of the American genius.

Thus cultural contacts with other groups were, with certain notable exceptions, kept at a minimum; the average American was so preoccupied with his personal problems and the conquest of his environment that he was scarcely aware of the existence of other ways of life.

Such inter-cultural attitudes as existed were generally stereotypes founded on history and tradition rather than impressions gained from direct personal contact.

These enabled the United States to remain relatively aloof from the mainsteams of international political life.

Americans came to feel that their non-involvement in the periodic crises of world affairs was due either to the excellence with which political and cultural matters were handled by the leaders of this country or to some form of moral preeminence that entitled them to receive favours from providence.

It became a mark of America's superior virtue and intelligence that the United States was able to play a lone hand in such international ventures as it undertook up to 1900; American ability to overlook or ignore the entirely fortuitous quality of this state of affairs was unlimited.

Indeed, American culture as it matured in the nineteenth century came to display most of the marks of a typical provincial society. Some of these were an exaggerated attachment to familiar places and social processes, a distrust of alien influence in any area of life, and inability or a refusal to learn new procedures from others or even to admit that there were any worth learning, a flaunting of the aspects of the culture of which we were the most proud (technological advance, industrial production, and a high standard of living are only three examples) as being conclusive proof of the merits of American culture, and—most subtly—the transformation of admitted weak points into concealed sources of strength.

This tendency to made virtues of one's own shortcomings is common in all provincial societies but is particularly marked in the United States. Thus American diplomatic failures (often the result of an unrealistic American public opinion) are excused on the ground that diplomacy is a dirty and tricky business, ill suited to the frank, open-hearted, honest, and uncomplicated American character. The relatively low standards of taste in the United States are explained away by semi-learned conclusions that literary and artistic creativity are marks of a decadent society; in a truly virile and healthy one, it is claimed, individual interest is centred more on building and creating material things of enduring value.

American Intercultural Contacts: The twentieth century, and particularly the period since 1945, has brought American culture, developed in relative isolation from other cultural streams and armed with a provincial distrust of all outsiders, into headlong and continuous contact with the rest of the world.

The realization that the rest of the world is not eagerly awaiting the opportunity to become just like the United States but that instead each group intends to follow its own line of cultural development has been a source of dismay and in some cases—lasting shock to many Americans. As a matter of fact, when we Americans realized in 1945 that the nineteenth century was forever gone, we made a sincere effort to grasp the implications of membership in the world society. The good intentions of the United States were real and, we thought, should have been obvious to all. We wished everyone well, the greatest boon that we know to confer on them was the opportunity, but diligent application and hard work, to take for themselves the salient features of American culture.

The Need for Intercultural Understanding. This new cynicism is unrealistic as was the earlier optimism. It was folly for Americans to expect all.

It is just as fatal in the long run, however, to assume a permanent lack of understanding between the rest of the world and ourselves.

Technology is not arrested simply because many Americans have had their feelings hurt; it goes on every day about it task of knitting the world more closely together. Our contacts are going to grow more numerous and every more intimate, and the world is with us to say.

A world of law and order in which orderly processes replace violence and fear can come about only after significant progress has been made toward the creation of a body of shared values among peoples in all states.

It can occur only as the result of a long process of many sided inter group contacts, in the course of which each culture borrows from the other. Each one acquires for itself such particular features as take root naturally and serve a desirable purpose, but maintains tolerance, sympathy, and understanding for such cultural differences as persist despite this intimate relationship. It is not the existence of cultural divergences that is the cause of international and inter-group tension, but rather the emotional reaction of peoples to the differences.

Unless we move in this direction, the United States will follow one of three courses: an unprofitable and ultimately futile isolationism, an uninformed and inept attempt to establish an American-created world authoritarianism under rigid control from the United States. None of these policies provides any assurance of success, but all are pregnant with danger. Any of them would lead us to a path of cultural development which might involve the steady and permanent surrender of the freedom that is such an integral part of human life course.

9

Towards World Order

With frequent increase in wars in severity as a result of man's increased mastery of technology and its application to the task of killing human beings, the urgency of the search for a device to free the world from this danger has increased. During the twentieth century, there have simultaneously taken place the most destructive wars of history and the most ambitious attempts to provide machinery to stabilize world relationships.

The 'race between education and catastrophe' in which many may feel our age is engaged in growing in intensity. With such grave issues at stake, the problems of world order move from the realm of philosophical speculation into the area of practical necessity.

Although the logic of interstate relations makes much the same demands upon governments as always and the same criteria of political success are applied to the pursuit of national interest by each state, a sensitive observer can search a theme in the current international scene. Many men express their dismay at the prospect of an unending series of increasingly destructive wars. Up to the present, this implicit cleavage between governments and their people has not major effect upon world politics. By and large, however, the growth of private resistance to the familiar nationalist stimuli has served to introduce a perceptible restraint into the calculations of statesmen, and the course of international affairs today reveals that different value systems are gaining some acceptance.

The populations of certain states formerly extremely active in world affairs than decided that many of their traditional objectives are no longer worth with effort, and they are instead casting about for some new method of achieving their fundamental goals. Such formerly nationalistic states as France and Italy, for example, have led the way toward European unification, a recommitment that draws its strength from a broadly based popular movement throughout Western Europe.

Wide rejection of the traditional basis for world politics being an unmistakable fact, it is no wonder that the interest of statesmen and scholars a like centres as never before about the search for world order. Yet the demand for peace is voiced so clearly and so emphatically by millions of individuals that statesmen do not dare let lapse their attempts to discover a permanent basis for international stability and peace.

The common objective of all the many proposals for world order, whether actually institutionalized or yet merely blue printed, is the elimination of the fundamental irresponsibility of states in their relations with one another. Independently of the semantic tyranny exercised by the world `sovereignty, what makes much of international politics unbearable for many people is that fact that states are ultimately accountable only to themselves. So long as no machinery exists to enforce the demand that they live in peace with each other states need fear no automatic sanctions if they break out into open war.

A central authority to prescribe modes of conduct for international life and with power to enforce them seems to millions the only way in which individuals can be assured of the minimal peace and stability they so ardently crave.

There are two general approaches to the core problem of the creation of such an agency. One method retains the nation-states as the basic unit of political organization and attempts to set up machinery with which states may work cooperatively for a more rational world order.

The other outlook assumes that as long as the nation-state exists, it is futile to third of peace; the dynamics of state life are such that the state institution will make inevitable the continuance of the disorder and crises that have been the lot of man. It, therefore, reject the nation-state and substitutes for it some variety of supra-national government into which the former states would fit as component parts. The distinction between the two methods of attack is more apparent than real, however. Many of the proponents of world government accept international organization on the order of the United Nations as the first step in the direction in which they desire to move, while the defenders of the idea of state-based international organization tend to agree that its evolution will be toward the transfer of real sovereignty in the central agency.

The two methods represent two stations along the same and, one somewhat farther along than the other. They differ from one another principally in the directness of their immediate attack upon national sovereignty.

THE LEAGUE OF NATIONS

The League of Nations was the first world agency to ponder over the gravity of war and its fatal consequences. International organization attempts to bring peace and order to world politics by engrafting upon the nation-state system a set of formalized institutions. This organizational framework is designed to serve two purposes.

It is intended to provide a framework within which world public opinion can be brought to bear upon issues, and a decision expressed that marinates from the consciences of individuals from all over the world. This 'world forum' is designed to make available a channel through which the will of the people—as apart from their official representatives and political leaders—can be expressed.

The machinery of international organization is so constructed as to permit states that wish to co-operate for peaceful purposes to do so more easily and efficiently.

Most of the perpetual crisis of international politics is due to the lack of an adequate institutional structure, forcing states to improvise techniques at a time when speedy action is vital to ward off disaster. The creation of machinery to be ready when needed enables states to concentrate directly upon the issue in hand.

This was the League of Nations, whose brief history was clouded by controversy, and even today judgment is far from unanimous in regard to its effectiveness or lack of it.

Historical Background

Though popularly associated in the American mind with the name of President Woodrow Wilson, the League of Nations was the culmination of a series of movements within the principal Allied states during the war. Organizations, including both private persons and government officials, had campaigned for a permanent international body to enforce peace. During 1916 and 1917, as the prospects for an Allied victory became more encouraging, the tempo of preparations for the League intensified. In United Kingdom, in France, and in the United States, government committees and influential private individuals were contributing their ideas to an evolving project, which was to culminate in the Covenant of the League. By the time of the America in 1918, President Wilson was the best-known advocate of the idea, but he was only the leader of an international movement of great size.

It was Wilson himself who insisted that the Covenant be an integral part of the peace security men's in 1919; his victory was demonstrated by the fact that the Covenant only became Part I of the Treaty of Versailles and all the other documents and made up the `Peace of Paris,' which brought the war to an end.

The history of the League is best told in phases. The first phase was the immediate post-war period, from 1919 to 1925. This era was marked by great controversy between the two principal members of the organization, France and Great Britain. The end of the war had released them from the common interest that had held them together, and their diverging policies found a convenient battleground in the League. France viewed the organization as an instrument for the perpetuation of its supremacy over Germany, this reflecting a continuing French concern with security; Britain, interested in securing a restoration of the balance of power and the limitation of the French hegemony in Europe, attempted to use the League for this purpose.

Their perpetual quarrel in the League and over the prostrate body of Germany marked the early years of the organization's history. This period reached its culmination in the French occupation of the Ruhr in 1924.

Reconciliation replaced the hatreds of the war era, the pact of

Locarno (1925) seemed to settle the troublesome issue of the German frontier in the west, and statesmen in Britain, France, and Germany sought to create a new atmosphere of cordiality and cooperation. Germany's entry into the League was a symbol of the liquidation of the old epoch and the entry into the new.

From 1925 to 1930, the League was the political centre of gravity. The world's leading statesmen congregated at Geneva, and decisions made there determined the course of world politics. World public opinion was phrased and articulated in the Assembly; great-power cooperation was a reality in the Council.

It seemed as if president Wison's dream was coming true and that the world had discovered the formula which would make peace in the world a permanent reality.

The Period of Decline: After 1930, however, the disruptive forces in world affairs took command and demolished this structure of cooperation. Two factors of almost equal importance contributed to the decline of the League in the 1930's: the first was the world-wide economic depression that began in 1929, and the second was the rise of fanatic nationalism.

The will to cooperate disappeared and with it went any prospects for the league. Events underscoring this changed circumstance followed each to the rapidly. In 1931 Japan committed aggression in Manchuria and withdrew from the League of Nations as opposition was voiced. In 1933 Hitler's Germany withdrew because France refused to grant arms equality. In 1935 Mussolini led his Fascist government of Italy out of the organization in a squabble over Italy's naked aggressions in Ethiopia. About the same time public confidence in the League was further weakened by the Spanish Civil War.

Even the admission into membership of the USSR in 1934 failed to galvanize the organization into action despite the ferment and apparently sincere efforts of the Soviet representative, Maxim Latency. By 1935 the League was completely in effective. The dictators had proved that no consequences would follow from outright defiance of the organization which had been supposed to be the embodiment of man's will to peace. The internal machinery remained in existence after this date, the members wringing their hands over the all-too-obvious approach of World War II but being unwilling or unable to take the necessary action, which alone could have staved off the coming disaster.

Organization and Functions

Membership: At its peak membership, in 1935, the League had sixty members. Sixty-two states joined at one time or another, but two had withdrawn, during the preceding ten years four states had been admitted; Germany, the USSR, Mexico, and Turkey. Germany and Japan withdrew officially in 1935, Italy shortly thereafter, and the USSR was expelled in 1940.

Of the twelve states generally recognized, as sovereign, which never assumed membership the United States, was the most important. Thus, it can be seen that the overwhelming majority of the sovereign political units of world politics between World Wars I and II at one time or another thought the League to be sufficiently important to merit membership.

Organization: The chief organs of the League were the Council and Assembly. The Assembly was the larger body, in which all members were entitled to representation and to one vote. It met regularly atleast once a year and in special sessions.

The Assembly was thought of as an advisory agency whose principal functions were the discussion of issues and the forming and articulating of World public opinion. Its area of competence was the entire scope of the covenant.

The Council of the League was a small body. The great powers were given permanent membership in it; a number of other states were elected by the Assembly to non-permanent seats. The number of non-permanent seats was steadily increased from the original four (this gave the great powers a permanent majority) to a high of eleven at the end. The Council was thought as the executive arm of the League, with the principal responsibility for the preservation or restoration of peace.

Certain other components of the League system enjoyed an importance of their own. The Secretariat of the League included experts in a great variety of technical fields whose duties were advisory and administrative.

The chief permanent officer of the League was the Secretary-

General, the administrative in world affairs: an international civil service whose responsibility was to the organization (and to the mass of humanity which it represented) instead of being confined to the peoples of a single state. The Secretariat set extremely high standards of loyalty and competence for any later group of similar nature to equal. Also parts of the pattern were the Permanent Court of International Justice (the World Court) and the International Labour Organization.

Functions: The first function involved taking action against short-term threats to the peace which might arise within the present structure of the nation-state system. This was thought to be the primary task of the Council, since it was more than anything else a problem of enforcement.

Included in these short-run functions were three broad areas of action, in each of which the League was charged with a definite mission land in each of which some action was taken during the few years of the organization's life.

The first was the responsibility placed upon the League for the pacific settlement of disputes. The record of accomplishment which it made, particularly before 1930, was not inconsiderable; several troublesome issues were removed from controversy by League intervention.

The second function, accomplished with much less success, was the creation of techniques of collective security. Several attempts were made to prescribe specific measures by which this elusive concept could become a reality within the League structure, including the Treaty of Mutual Assistance (1923), the Geneva Protocol (1924), and the General Act of 1928. None of these attained any success, though the General Act cleared the League machinery and was thrown open to accession by any state. By 1935 only about twenty states had joined, and these were insufficient both in number and in power to make a real collective security system. The most elaborate collective security measure of the interwar period was drawn up and signed outside the League; this was the Kellogg-Briand Pact (1928), which affirmed the renunciation of war as an instrument of national policy.

The history of the League efforts at `disarmament' is long, fussing, and depressing tale into which there is no need to go at this time. The governments of the member states, particularly the great powers, never became convinced that their national interest would emit any substantial over-all reduction in military preparedness, however riding any of them might be to have their opponents disarm. The short-range functions of the League were coupled with several of ledger purview. These are commonly termed the `non-political' areas of acids of the interwar period looking to the satisfaction of the private demands of individuals. Yet this economic, social, and psychological programme of the League had distinct political connotation. Its target was the amelioration of the conditions of human existence which produce social problems that are themselves breeding grounds for war.

No more hopeful method of ultimately eliminating war from human society exists than that of cooperative programmes to provide the rewards which societies otherwise seek to take by force.

This idea was only imperfectly understood the drafters of the Covenant, and the League's organization for economic and social activity was incomplete and, to a considerable extent, extemporized.

Three principal organizations were established within the League structure to deal with particular areas: the Economic and Financial Organization, the Communications and Transit Organization, and the Health Organization. All of the autopsies which various authors have performed upon the defunct League of Nations agree that this area of League activity was the most successful, even though it was of insufficient scope to make any impression upon the political and security problems that crippled the organization.

Reasons for the Failure of the League

The United States, Soviet Russia, and Germany were not original members. Germany was taken in 1926; the Soviet Union joined in 1934, but by that time, the League was weakened by the withdrawal of Germany and Japan. The United States never accepted membership.

Thus the League was always handicapped by an obvious lack of agreement among the very powers whose active cooperation was nickering to its success. Even among the great powers whose membership was interrupted or uninterrupted there was a constant confusion of motivation.

United Kingdom (Britain) repeatedly attempted to employ the League as an instrument of the balance of power. France concentrated upon Germany and sought to use the League to guarantee French security.

Germany, on the other, attempted through the Leaguer to escape from the onus placed upon it by the Treaty of Versailles; the German people eventually chose the Nazi way of attaining this end. There was also a constant operational difficulty inherent within the structure of the organization. The small states were then (as now) very vehement in their formulation of the ideal of international organization and wished through the League to gain protection against the depredations of any of the great powers. They soon became impatient at the pretensions of the major states to control of the League. They seized control of the Assembly, and amended the structure of the Council to give them a majority in that body.

The Members of the League were quite clear and specific that they had not given up their sovereign independence when they entered upon their membership. Membership was voluntary and the right of withdrawal was guaranteed. This meant in practice that effective action by the organization was contingent upon an identity of interest among the members.

So long as no serious and fundamental conflicts of interest developed the League survived and, as we have seen, during the period of confidence of interest the League prospered. However, as soon as Japan, Italy, Germany, and the USSR (in the Finish war of 1940-41) chose each in its turn to `go it alone.' The key members proved unwilling to take the requisite action to stop them.

Behind all the organizational faults of the Leagues lies a more fundamental factor in its failure. The League largely owed its creation to a popular revulsion against power politics and its refreshment wars. The pressures of the postwar period—economic crisis, social infection, the weakness of political democracy—undermined the commitment of millions of people to the ideal of a warless world epitomized by the League. Instead, various forms of intransigent nationalism came to serve as the dominant force in world public opinion.

This enabled political leaders, who for a while had been forced by public pressure to co-operate with each either almost against their will, again too calculate policy upon the familiar beds of the free-wheeling concept of unrestrained national interest.

The League collapsed ignominiously in the cauldron of World War II, and in the minds of most of mankind it represents one of man's complete failures. That it was a failure is undeniable; after all, if an organization designed to preserve the peace is wiped out by a global war involving its members, we can scarcely assert that the organization was a success.

Its brief period of existence did contain promise of eventual good and provided several lessons for future generations. It afforded many people proof that the basic idea of international organisation had vitality and validity.

The League also furnished the inspiration and example of an international civil service in the Secretariat. This group of technically trained experts whose primary loyalty was to the organization provided the international point of view in contrast to the more narrow nationalist orientation brought to the organization by the representatives of states. This idea was transferred bodily to the United Nations.

THE UNITED NATIONS

As World War II was drawing to a close, there was no doubt in the minds of the leaders of the principal Allied nations that some new venture in international cooperation was going to be undertaken to replace the League of Nations.

The heritage of the League itself was, as has been pointed out, not inconsiderable, furthermore, such good results had been attained during the war by permanent political consultation at a high level that the perpetuations of this practice was felt to be indispensable to a permanent peace.

The war time United Nations Organization (UNO)—the fighting alliance—served as the organizational base upon which was erected the postwar United Nations. It is an eloquent tribute to the force of the idea of international organization that even the failure and discrediting of the League did not dampen popular under for a renewal of the system.

Creation: The United Nations formally came into being on 24 October 1954. The Charter itself had been completed and signed several months earlier at San Francisco. Representatives of fifty governments approved the document at that time.

This action was a culmination of years of work by many people, which made possible the calling of the Untied Nations Conference on International Organization (UNCIO), at which the final form of Charter was determined. The preparatory steps were innumerable, both within the various member state of the military alliance and at the international level. The progress toward the realization of the idea of the United Nations was perhaps epitomized by the several great international conferences during the war, at each one of which some new point was announced which brought the emerging organization one step nearer completion.

The initial moment at which it could definitely be said that a commitment in favour of a postwar international organization had been made was the Moscow Conference of foreign ministers, in the autumn of 1943. Here the United States, Great Britain, the Soviet Union and China agreed to the principle of the establishment of a general international organization at the earliest practicable date.

This was almost immediately reinforced by the statement that was issued following the Teheran Conference of Roosevelt, Churchill, and Stalin, in which the 'Big Three' promised that they personally would initiate action to such purpose. In July 1944, the Bretton Woods Conference for postwar economic and financial stability drew up agreements establishing the World Bank and the World Monetory Fund. That autumn there convened the most important preliminary step prior to UNCIO itself, the Dumbarton Oaks Conference. Here China, Great Britain, the USSR, and the United States drew up a draft proposal for the structure of the organization which served as the basis for action at San Francisco.

At the Yalta Conference, in February 1945, Roosevelt, Churchill, and Stalin agree upon a voting formula in the Security Council (the famous 'veto') and formally called UNCIO to convene in San Francisco on 25 April 1945.

The San Francisco Conference operated primarily upon the basis of the Dumbarton was subject to several fundamental amendments and considerable elaboration.

The greatest departure from the original draft was in the significant expansion the conference made in the economic and social activities of the organization, including the Trusteeship Council and the specifying of the functions of the Economic and Social Council. It was clear that the familiar quarrel between the great powers and the small states was going to be renewed in the new organization; at San Francisco many attempts were made to weaken the privileged role that the major states had taken upon themselves. Most of these were unsuccessful and the final form of the Charter was in general conformity to the ideas of the 'Big Four', who had carried the bulk of the load of the war.

The General Assembly: The General Assembly is, like the Assembly of the League which preceded it, the one organ in which all members are represented. Each state has one vote and up to five representatives. Its primary function, within the original intent of the Charter, is to serve as the sounding board for world public opinion and to supervise the economic and social work of the organization.

It is not given any power to take action upon substantive matters as is the Security Council; it operates by means of recommendations and advice to national states and to the Security Council. In one sense, its role is more sharply circumscribed than was that of the League Assembly. It is debarred from considering any question already before the Security Council as long as the later chooses to keep the matter on its agent. This was admittedly an attempt on the part of the large states holding permanent seats on the Security Council to prevent the Assembly (in which the small states would clearly be dominant) from forcing the hand of the great powers.

As matters have worked out, however, the General Assembly has not been kept in such a subordinate role. The hamstringing of the Security Council by the Great Power dispute between the East and the West has made the General Assembly the centre of the United Nations system. What make this peculiarly significant is the voting formula in the Assembly, which includes a clear break in the historic rule of unanimity. On 'important' questions a two-thirds majority of all those present and voting is sufficient, while on all other a simple majority is adequate. In this way a real rupture was made in the principle of 'sovereign equality' upon which the

Charter claims the organization is based. A state that votes 'no' on a question may be outvoted and thus be bound against its will.

The Security Council: The Security Council is charged with 'primary responsibility' for the maintenance of international peace and security and was originally thought of as the only organ of the United Nations which would be powerful enough to take affirmative action in this direction. It consists of eleven members and is in continuous session.

Five states hold permanent membership on the Council: Great Britain, France, the USSR (Russia), the United States, and China; the remaining six are elected by the General Assembly for two-years terms.

The Security Council has authority over all international disputes which may be referred to it, and it may take action in any `threat to the peace, breach of the peace, or act of aggression.' It is empowered to impose a variety of methods of pacific settlement upon disputing states; in the event of defiance by an aggressor it may impose punitive sanctions, including the employment of such armed forces as the members are pledged to provide. The council also has authority to initiate action looking toward the reduction and limitation of armaments. The 'veto' exists only in the Security Council. It appears as part of the Charter provision which stipulates voting procedure in that body.

Decisions in the Security Council on procedural matters require affirmative votes of seven members; decisions on 'all other matters' require affirmative votes of seven members 'including the occurring votes of the permanent members.'

The Economic and Social Council: The Economic and Social Council can best be thought of as a standing committee of the General Assembly which is primarily responsible for the execution of the parent body's mission in this field. It consists of eighteen states elected by the General Assembly or three years. It supervises most of the geographic and functional commissions of the United Nations.

The Trusteeship Council: The Trusteeship Council has a general grant of power over non-self-governing territories and especially over the United Nations 'trusteeships' scattered throughout the world. These trusteeships are of three types: those taken over from the League mandate system, territories taken from the Axis powers as a result of World War II, and other non-self-governing territories voluntarily placed under the system.

Membership on the Trusteeship Council is granted to three categories of states: members administering trust territories, permanent members of the Security Council who do not administer trust territories, and sufficient other states elected by the General Assembly to make a balance between trustee states and non-trustee states.

The International Court of Justice: The fifth of the 'principal organs' of the United Nations is the International Court of Justice. This body the direct descendant of the Permanent Court International Justice, is an integral part of the United Nations and its Statute is included as part of the Charter.

The Secretariat. The Secretariat is named after the similar group, which provided continuity for the League. The Secretary-General is the head of the Secretariat and is the chief administrator for the entire organization. He is empowered to take certain initiatory action in bringing before the Security Council matter that might threaten international peace and security. He is assisted by a staff drawn from all the members of the United Nations, whose function is to provide technical, administrative, and clerical assistance to the remainder of the organization.

Improvements on the League

Membership: As the statesmen of the world, spurred on by public opinion, approached the creation of the United Nations, they were determined to correct some of the more glaring shortcomings of the League of Nations. A first improvement over the League was a more inclusive membership.

Thanks to wartime unity, there were no significant absentees from the organization. All of the states which at the end of the war, possessed any appreciable amount of power were included among the original members; only the defeated Axis and certain minor states were excluded.

The United States and the drafting of the Charter, and an

implicit understanding was reached that as each of the defeated former enemies could qualify, it would also be accepted into membership. Universality of membership was the goat at which the framers were aiming.

The Security Council and the Veto: The struggle between Council and Assembly, between large states and small, was minimized. As we have seen, the security council was given a monopoly of authority over crises and all disputes that menaced the peace.

It is true that the veto has served for Americans as the principle symbol of the frustration to which the United Nations has subjected them, and much opposition has been voided to the whole idea.

Two comments on the veto might be made at this point. In the first place, under the League rule of complete unanimity before any action could be taken, every state had a veto. The number is now reduced to five, this is at least a step in the right direction. In the second place, without the veto there would have been no United Nations at all. The record of UNCIO shows clearly that the point was sufficiently important to the USSR (and to the United States as well) that no agreement was possible and no organization would have been created had not the privileged position of the great power been recognized in this way.

The Security Council was thus safely in the hands of the permanent members, who bore primary responsibility for enforcing the peace. On the other hand, the new `forum'—the General Assembly—was given the power to reach conclusions and to make recommendations by far less than unanimity, and there is no veto in the General Assembly.

This, it was hoped, would make the larger body even more responsive to currents of world opinion than its predecessor had been.

Other Improvements: Many other technical improvements over the League can be found in the Charter. One is the creation of the Economic and Social Council, with the special mission of coordination all the non-political activity of the United Nations.

Another is the inclusion of the International Court of Justice within the organization, thus making all United Nations members *ipso facto* adherents to the Statute of the court.

The Place of the United Nations in World Politics Today

Where does the United Nations stand today? Feelings run high when an answer to this question is attempted, and no general summary is possible that would satisfy everyone. One proposition, however, is virtually self-evident.

The United Nations has once again demonstrated that international organization, in and of itself, is no panacea for the ills of the world.

The present organization remains merely a framework within which states may co-operate more effectively. If the will to do so is not present, the framework is useless because it is unused.

The cold war has paralyzed much of the activity of the United Nations but the fault, if fault there be, rests with the foreign policies of the states themselves.

So long as the essential quality of the nation-state system is preserved (Article 2, paragraph 1 of the Charter says: `The Organization is based on the principle of the sovereign equality of all its Members') the determining factor of international politics will continue to be the sovereign will of the nation-state.

Popular Support: In attempting to strike a balance upon the role of the United Nations in world politics today, a valid starting point is the question of popular support. Despite its inability to revolutionize international relations and the occasional frustrations which result, the United Nations has taken a remarkable grip upon the hopes and the outlook of the great masses of people all over the world. This is particularly true among the smaller states, many of which are recently removed from colonial or dependent status. The result of the trust that so many people place in the United Nations has been the creation of a tremendous moral force rooted in mass opinion, which statesmen must perforce recognize.

Even the Soviet Union is actually very much aware of the prestige that accrues to the United Nations and is vehement in its public professions of support, regardless of what its record of action may indicate. Though the voices of those who have lost faith (or who never really had any) may be shrill, much of mankind sees in the United Nations the symbol of what it wants the world of the future to be. This is of profound significance today.

At a time when so much stress is being placed upon the dramatic devices of power politics and when international relations are conducted in an atmosphere of constant tension, there is a perceptible resistance by millions of people to the divisive pull of hysterical nationalism and a tendency to look toward the goal of a world without war.

It would be stupid to assert flatly that the verdict of man today is in favour of co-operation and that war is obsolete.

But it would be equally fatuous to pretend that a global will to peace does not exist or to presume that the impact of world opinion upon international politics is of no effect and that the historic penetrable—interest, policy, and power—have remained unmodified.

Successes of the United Nations: Barring the primary days, UNO has proved failure, particularly during last decade when after the collapse of USSR, it could not check over ambition of the USA.

All during the period of relative international stalemate that followed the end of the war in 1954, the organizational machinery has kept working and in the process the members have gained a great deal of facility in its operation.

The improvement in the climate of world noted by many observers following the 'summit' conference at Geneva in July 1955, raised hopes that the long-sought policy reconciliation between the two major adversaries in world politics was now a possibility. If it were to come about, the United Nations would become a truly effective instrument for world cooperation.

Procedures in the United Nations have already become standardized, the Secretariat has been assembled and trained, the outlines of the continuing tasks of the organization have been clearly delineated, and much preparatory technical and administrative data on them are already assembled. The survival of the United Nations through darkest days of cold war augurs well for its future.

But the organization also has a short but significant record of successes. As part of its duty to keep the peace, it has intervened in several international quarrels.

Other controversies in which United Nations intervention was prompt and in which such action made major contributions toward the eventual pacific settlement include the Soviet-Iranian quarrel in 1946, the Kashmir dispute between India and Pakistan and roughly a dozen of lesser significance.

Many people have voiced the criticism that in these disputes the United Nations has been unable to produce definitive solutions and has therefore failed in its mission, but such attacks betray ignorance of the theory and functions of the organization. It was never intended that the United Nations would either solve or eliminate all interstate conflicts; only a world government would have the power to do that, and it is clear that the United Nations is not a world government.

Also to the credit of the organization should be placed a number of less visible entries. These are the international quarrels that have not gone to the point of endangering international peace and security because the disputants realized that any such action would bring the United Nations into the picture. We have no way of knowing how many such there are, but that the intense controversy of the postwar world has produced many we can be sure.

In many ways this effect of the United Nations is its greatest success. If it can, by its existence along, serve to deflect the course of international conflict into peaceful channel, no greater level of attainment can be asked of it.

The Korean Intervention: Of course, the most courageous step taken in the name of the United Nations up to the present time was the intervention into the Korean war. Although the confusion of motives among them membership was apparent at the time the action was taken, there is no escaping the central fact that for the first time in history the members of an international organization supported an abstract principle with arms and men. It is true that the action was taken in the absence of the Soviet Union and that the full co-operation assumed by the organization was not present; following the USSR's return to the Security Council further action there proved to be impossible.

The 'Uniting for peace' resolutions of 1950, however, provided that if the Security Council was unable to reach a decision on a security question because of a veto or for any other reason, the General Assembly was authorized to assume jurisdiction over the question.

Accordingly, further steps in the prosecution of the war and, after the truce of July 1953, the preparation for the post-hostilities political conference were undertaken by the General Assembly. Despite the intrusion of narrow formulations of national interest into a question of collective security, the Korean issue carries one clear moral. The great majority of the population of the world, speaking through their representatives, registered their decision that aggression by violence should not go undressed regardless of the cost and the danger.

As we have seen it, it was a lack of this willingness to hazard the unpredictable in the pursuit of an ideal, which really brought about the decay and collapse of the League. It is obvious today that many of the states that intervened in Korea did so about whether or not a principle was involved. Indeed, president Truman asserted that this was so in the case of the United States.

It is nevertheless clear that many states have greatly broadened their idea of national interest to comprehend the idea that everyone's best interest is served by peaceful change.

It will be easier to do the same thing another time, but the likelihood of having to do it again is reduced, The more the members of the United Nations are willing to fight to keep the peace, the less danger there is of their having to do so.

Failures of the United Nations: The United Nations has failed to live up to the expectations of many of its supporters. One major failure may be fairly charged to the organizational, as well as several lesser ones that derive from it.

The central inadequacy demonstrated by the United Nations since its inception has been its inability to cope with the cold war.

The near-total refusal made by United States and the USSR to any proposals involving cooperative action within the organization's scope has paralyzed action in the direction of collective security and world peace and has seriously inhibited programmes in all other fields.

American particularly are inclined to contend that the lack of success of the United Nations in dealing with Soviet obstructionism is a proof that the Organization is a failure; we point to the success of the Soviet in applying the veto to proposals aimed at halting communism and many of us claim that the inability of the United Nations to serve as an instrument of American policy vitiates the usefulness of the entire organization.

Regardless of the merit of the American case, it is clear that no international organization of which the Soviet Union (or, for that matter, any major power) is a member can be turned into a instrument against it. The framers of the Charter were realists; they realized that unless great-power cooperation for peace was a reality, there was no use creating any organization to embody such an idea.

Therefore, it is a real criticism of the United Nations to point out that it has been unable to end the cold war with a victory for the United States, but it is not a just one. The organization was not built for any such purpose and to expect it to do so is unwarranted.

Just as the problem of the solution of the cold war must be returned to the states involved, so may most of the other shortcomings of the United Nations. The `spirit' of the organization has not come up to the hopes of its framers. States still tend to consider the United Nations just another vehicle of policy, to be used when appropriate, to be defied when necessary, and to be ignored when other techniques are more expedient. The success of the United Nations idea necessitates that it be the centre around which other areas of international life range themselves. It has not been such a center; many of the most important problems of the postwar era have been worked out without ever being brought before either the Security Council or the General Assembly.

Demand for the Abolition of the Veto: Suggestions abound for improvements in United Nations procedure. The most common proposal deals with the abolition of the veto. This idea, most prevalent in the United States, springs from the fact that the Soviet Union has made vigorous use of it on the Security Council. Unanimity among the permanent members being lacking, action becomes impossible.

Of course, the United States and the other permanent members of the Security Council have also employed the veto, but all except France have avoided the necessity of being the only one in the negative. France unilaterally cast a negative vote on one occasion.

Schemes to abolish the veto invoke the principle of majority rule and envisage the happy state of the organization when the USSR would no longer be able to prevent action by the majority—particularly when that majority is led by the United States. Such arguments tend to overlook both legal technicalities and the realities of world politics.

Charter amendment is possible, but no amendment is effective unless it is approved by all permanent members of the Security Council. In other words, the Soviet Union has a veto on the question of the abolition of the veto. The USSR would approve such an amendment only if and when it felt it no longer needed the protection of the veto.

Within the inherent limitations of an organization of sovereign states the United Nations has justified its existence and the more realistic hopes of its framers and early supporters. It has proved to be powerless either to halt the cold war or to force a decision in it, but in theory and in operation it was not intended to deal with such a far-reaching controversy between two of its key members. When the 'agreement to disagree' of the two great camps has not been operative, the United Nations has proved to be an effective instrument for settling disputes. Its attack upon the long-range causes of war, epitomized in the Economic and Social Council, has not been under way long enough to provide sufficient information upon which to base a reasoned verdict, but there are some grounds for cautious optimism.

WORLD GOVERNMENT

Two major subgroups can be distinguished within the general classification of proposals for world government.

One school of thought argues that such a single-headed world government can be established only by conquest and the attainment of hegemony over the whole world by a single state; the other contends rather than by democratic action and a system of federation man can establish a peaceful world order under law.

The Hegemony School

The believers in hegemony approach the problem of world organization equipped with a keen sense of history and a pessimistic opinion of the capabilities of the human species for rational action. Historically, they argue that during those periods when mankind enjoyed the closest approximation to universal peace, the world was ruled by a single strong power. Sometimes the single state was a universal empire, as was Rome; sometimes the relationship of ruler and ruled was just as real although less formal, as in the case of the *Pax Brittanica* of the nineteenth century. They point to the diminution in the number of great powers today as proof of their thesis that another period of such peace and other is in the offing, lacking only the final great struggle for supremacy and the emergence of a single ruling state to bring it into existence. They reject the claims to independent policy by the minor members of the two great present-day alliances as well as denying that any state can remain neutral in such a struggle. They feel that man is incapable of exercising the systematic self-denial necessary to create the rule of law in the world, asserting instead that he will abide by the moral code only when driven to it by superior force. Thus, they content that by preaching the doctrine of conquest they are seeking only the best interest of individual men; by establishing peace based upon subjugation they are attempting to save man from himself. As might be expected, the idea of world government through hegemony is most popular with the states that consider themselves eminently qualified for the task of world rule. This has made the idea quite acceptable with one after another of the great powers of recent times.

Hitler, Mussolini, and the Black Dragon Society in Japan all predicted a future in which all mankind would live in happy unity under their benign rule.

Soviet Hegemony: The Soviet dream of world organization envisage a world freed from the `blight' of capitalism and therefore united into one social its brotherhood. The form of government adopted everywhere would be them of the `people's democracy,' a political system with which the Western would has already gained a certain familiarity.

The leaders of these governments would be in turn co-ordinate by a central directorate of the Communist party, dominated, of course, from Moscow.

No opposition would exist any where to the accomplishment of Russian objectives. War would be unknown since it is a capitalist invention; poverty, disease, and ignorance would be abolished; happiness and plenty would be the lot of man.

Whether the peoples of the world, who had interested in peace now, would subscribe to this programme with much ensign as is a proposition that is at best debatable.

American Hegemony: American proponents of the idea present much the same plan but from the point of view of the United States. Contending this `the American century,' and anachronistically contemplating the `civilizing mission' of the United States, they call for a great effort by our people to save the human race from the clutches of communist propaganda and the consequences of its own slothfulness and decay. Instead of the world-wide exportation of Soviet ideology, American thinkers conceive of a works made happy by universal acceptance of American economic and scientific organization, social values, cultural apparatus, political system, and military leadership.

Criticism to the Doctrine of Hegemony: These visions are extremely flattering to the hypertension nationalism of the state proposing them, but it is difficult to take them seriously. One would hardly expect the peoples ruled by the dominating power cheerfully to accept their permanent role of interact justifying the particular state's claim to rule upon a variety of grounds. Is cladding superiority of culture, intelligence, virility, or virtue.

To the `lesser' peoples whose destiny it is to be ruled by the all-powerful state, accepting any such argument necessitates their agreement with an unfavourable verdict upon their own culture and capacity for self-rule. Understandably, most so cities are reluctant on this score. Under the present conditions of world politics, the attempt to relax would involve the state concerned in a desperate struggle with all the peoples whose liberty it was seeking to extinguish. It claims that it was acting in good faith and with a primary interest in the welfare of individuals everywhere would be greeted by derision and resistance.

Critics of the 'peace through hegemony' school also point out how fatally and it is for a powerful state to rationalize a policy of aggrandizement and precession under the lofty pretensions of bring order and civilization to the add. It is historically true that the universal empires of the past were shout into existence by armed conquest, but these structures were generally all upon populations who did not have the highly developed sense of nationalism which characterizes contemporary political life.

The Federation School

On the contrary from the theory of hegemony is the proposal to form a international world government by the free act of peoples and their government. This theory has a long history, but it has gained the most adherents and the greatest momentum in the period since World War II. Concern with the probable consequences of any future war and with what they feel to be the findness of contemporary political leadership has bought many people in the Western World to the conclusion that the nation-state is obsolete. They agree that technology and social organization have progressed to the point were national states and their programmes of action are increasingly dangers to modern man as well as being inefficient in the solution of his problems.

Although varying in degree, all proposals put forth by people who share in belief involve a transfer of sufficient increments of national sovereignty in a new international agency to create a real world government with power enforce organization, which, as we have seen, is based upon the tributary co-operation of sovereign states. World government of this type of members, and it can therefore come about only when public sentiment has progressed to the point of being willing to make the emotional sacrifice adamant upon any such transfer of loyalty.

The government could be empowered to make law within certain prescribed grants of competence and would have power to enforce its decisions upon individuals and states.

Among the subjects upon which law could be made would in the whole question of interstate relations and the disputes arising. War would be flatly prohibited, the conduct in interstate intercourse subject to fixed rules, and violators liable to swift punishment.

Generally the federal government would also be granted auxiliary powers necessary to the performance of its primary mission.

Minimal Federation: This far all proposals for federation are in substantial agreement. As more details are filled in by the various groups, however, major divergences appear and at least two distinct points of view are apparent. One, here termed the minimal, looks upon world government almost as a necessary evil, and projects its proposals upon the basis of granting the new function of keeping the peace: most commonly this includes the maintenance of armed forces and the financial powers necessary to sustain them. This approach accepts cultural diversity as the normal lot of man and indeed sees much positive good in the nation-state as the embodiment of political community. The grouping of men into units to which they owe primary allegiance is preserved: states are urged to preserve maximum autonomy over local affairs. The major purpose of the organization is the negative one of preventing the state system from destroying itself by war. This is the general attitude of such groups as the United World Federalists in the United States.

Another form of minimal federalism accepts the preservation of the maximum of state autonomy as desirable and makes the prevention of war the major objective of any world government, but recognizes in addition that it would be advantageous for the central authority to act also in certain affirmative ways to the mutual benefit of all members.

Included in this area of added power would be such economic functions as a world currency, world free trade, and world control over the distribution of raw materials; such social powers as the provision of a single world bill of rights and the elevation of educational standards; such cultural operations as the removal of lowering of linguistic barriers.

The individuals who advocate that such authority be delegated to a world government are acutely sensitive to the example of the United States in the eighteenth century. The Constitution also contained affirmative provisions which have served as the vehicle for effective action in the common interest.

Whether purely negative or somewhat more positive in orientation, the first group of federalists is distinguished by its desire to retain the practical maximum of state autonomy and cultural diversity.

Maximal Federation: The other approach to world government may be termed maximalism or cosmopolitanism. A sizable group of dedicated, scholarly people in the United States and Europe, adopting as their own the classic stoic concept of the brotherhood of man and the commonwealth of the rational, seeks to destroy all boundaries that divide man into hostile groups, be they economic, political, or cultural.

Criticism of Cosmopolitanism: One cannot help but admire the grandeur of the vision of the plan of world cosmopolitanism and the weight of sound historical, anthropological, and psychological evidence that is adduced in its favour. Scientific studies demonstrate that men are basically alike and that cultural differences and nationalist hatreds and learned rather than instinctive.

This approach is not the vapid dream of impractical idealists. It is backed by some of the most reputable scientific arguments man can muster. Yet to condemn national states and nationalist sentiments as irrational does not eliminate them from existence.

Men are obstinately wedded to their prejudices; it will require more than mere exhortation to persuade them to abandon the ways of their fathers and to strike out in a drastically different direction. The major hostile criticism of the cosmopolitan approach is aimed at its insistence that immediate far-reaching action is necessary. It is at least possible to conceive of man's becoming a citizen of the world by the gradual process of progressively broadening his horizons.

Approaches to the Achievement of Federation

Immediate Action: Mention of the tactics used by the advocates of cosmopolitanism to obtain mass support introduces another aspect of the whole issue of federalism. The method by which some such plan might gain adoption has engaged much of the attention of the supporters of the idea. Initially the movement gathered momentum as a result of mass revulsion against, and fear of, another war and its consequences. Immediately after World War II in the United States and in Europe, organizations interested in world government sought to capitalize on this popular fear by telling people of the horrors of atomic war that would come unless they proceeded forthwith to form a federal world government.

Today the only group that seriously argues in favour of the immediate abolition of national sovereignty is the cosmopolitans, and we have seen that much of the urgency of their proposals is a tactical device to stimulate mass interest.

Other Methods: This means that there are actually two broad routes by which world government might be attained. One capitalizes upon the experience of the United Nations and proposes conferring upon it grants of real legislative and executive power. The other looks instead to the already strong trend toward the creation of supra- national governmental units upon a regional basis.

The United Nations Approach: It is an established fact that the United Nations, even with its limited and fiduciary powers, is able to meet and solve many problems of international life.

The organization particularly the General Assembly, has already undertaken projects of a distinctly legislative nature which tend to affect individuals in their daily lives—an omen of federalism in the making. Such broad ventures as the Universal Declaration of Human Rights and such willingness to pierce the barrier of national sovereignty as was demonstrated in the question of the Indian minority in the Union of South Africa indicate that much thinking is going on within the United Nations tending inevitably toward its evolution into a true agency of world government.

The Regional Approach: Regional federation among states who share common problems that can best be solved by the creation of common agencies is a trend that has impressed many observers with its promise since World War II.

Thus, it would be easier for a regional agency to build up popular confidence in the idea of a federal form by the accumulation of a record of success.

The Lessons of Europe: The lesson of the European experiment in unification is of widespread application. Despite the urgency and obvious appropriateness of some such procedure. Nationalist and traditionalist forces have made it impossible to transfer any sovereignty to a multi-purpose regional government for Europe.

Problems of Organization

Representation: Countless technical points intrude into the discussions of the details of the proposed forms of world government. Whether the world legislature should be unicameral or bicameral, with one house representing the state and the other the people as in the United States; whether the executive should be single (a 'President of the World') or plural; the method of selection of the executive, by world popular election or by means of some indirect technique; whether or not there should be a world judiciary to which cases could be appealed from national courts; the location of the world capital: all these are hotly debated.

Of much more basic character is the dispute over the proposed basis of representation. Since individuals as well as states would be represented in any such organization, the question of the basis upon which such representation would be apportioned in naturally of critical importance.

Literacy, wealth, and 'civilization' have been advanced as suggested criteria to modify that crude impact of sheer numbers in the legislative organ of any proposed world government.

A recent proposal entails the grouping of all states in three broad categories and the assignment of a fixed number of seats to all state within any category. For example, China, India, the USSR, and the United States, as `large' states, might each be assigned twenty seats; Great Britain, France, Indonesia, and Pakistan would all be `medium' seats with ten seats apiece; `small' states, such as Belgium, Canada, and Burma, would be content with five places.

The whole discussion reveals a problem inherent in the nature of the movement for world government. The idea grows out of Western political experience, where a common culture provides a rational base for representation by population. When applied to the entire world, the very proponents of the idea discover that they (and the culture they represent) would be in a hopeless minority compared to the masses who do not understand representative institutions.

Democracy: This problem has an even deeper root. Unless the point of view of the proponents of world hegemony is accepted, any world government must be constructed upon a democratic basis.

The fundamental concepts common to all proposals for federation are integral parts of the democratic idea: limited government, separation of powers, popular election of officials, universal suffrage, and natural rights. Democracy as a working principle depends upon a moral consensus among the people who are to be governed. Unless this basic agreement exists, democratic forms are perverted and the system becomes a sham.

The communist 'people's democracy' illustrates such a prostitution of popular government. Until the underlying democratic concept that everyone abides by majority decisions in good faith is understood and accepted by people everywhere, the establishment of a structure of world government would be useless and dangerous.

Can the world be organized on the basis they propose in time to stave off the catastrophe of another war which might mean the end of our civilization? is the fundamental question.

If the race to save the world is to be won, it will be only as a result of the extension of the democratic idea and the perfecting of the machinery of federalism. Given the instability of international politics and the ever-present possibility of a resort to war, it is easy to become pessimistic and resigned to disaster. It may very well be that man has a little more time in which to develop new political forms and techniques than some people have been willing to grant him.

There is little doubt that the broad trend of history is toward some form of organization transcending the nation-state. The only question is whether social development will progress rapidly enough to effect the change in sufficient time. The optimum basis of political organization is determined at any point in history by a variety of factors. The two most important of these are the maximum area it is technologically feasible to govern from a single seat of power and the maximum area within which the people feel themselves united into a single nation.

Cross-culture, free world trade, and recent developments in the direction of 'world a global village' like steps will definitely lead to a world governement if sincere efforts are made. Today the development of transportation and communication has made it possible to govern efficiently with whole world as a constituency. All that is lacking is the extension of the concept of the nation into something broader that will encompass the whole of humankind.

Bibliography

Apter, David, *The Gold Coast in Transition*, Princeton: Princeton University Press, 1955.

Armstrong, John A., "Sources of Administrative Behaviour: Some Soviet and Western European Comparisons," *The American Political Science Review*, LIX, 3 (September 1965), 643-55.

Beard, Charles A., *The Idea of National Interest*, New York: Macmillan, 1934.

Benedict, Ruth, *The Chrysanthemun and the Sword*, Boston Houghton Mifflin, 1946.

Boulding, Kenneth A., *Conflict and Defence*, New York: Harper & Row, 1962.

Brodie, Bernard, *Strategy in the Missile Age*. Princeton: Princeton University Press, 1959.

Cobden, Richard, *Political Writings*, New York: Appleton, 1867, Vol. I.

Crozier, Brian, *The Rebels*, London: Chatto and Windus, 1960.

Dahl, Robert A., "A Critique of the Ruling Elite Model," *The American Political Science Review*, LII, 2(June 1958), 463-69.

Deutsch, Karl W., and J. David Singer, "Multipolar Systems and International Stability," *World Politics*, XVI, 3(April 1964), 390-406.

Deutsch, Karl, *The Nerves of Government*, New York: Free Press 1963.

Eisenstadt, S.N., *Modernization: Protest and Change*, Englewood Cliffs, N.J.: Prentice-Hall, 1966.

Frankel, Herbert S., *The Economic Impact on Underdeveloped Societies*, Cambridge: Harvard University Press, 1953.

Galuson, Walter, *Labour Productivity in Soviet and American Industry*, New York: Columbia University Press, 1955.

Hayes, Carleton J., *The Historical Evaulation of Modern Nationalism*, New York: R.R. Smith, 1931.

Hertz, Frederick, *Nationality in History and Politics*, New York: Oxford University Press, 1944.

Hoffman, Stanley, ed. *Contemporary Theory of International Relations*, Englewood Cliffs, N.J.: Prentice-Hall, 1960.

Hurewitz, J.C., *Middle East Dilemma*, New York: Harper & Row' 1953.

Janowitz, Morris, *The Military in the Political Development of New Nations*, Chicago: The University of Chicago Press, 1964.

Johnson, Chalmers, *Revolutionary Chanve*, Boston: Little, Brown, 1966.

Kaplan, Morton, A "Balance of Power, Bipolarity, and other Models of International Systems," *The American Political Science Review*, LI, 3(September 1957), 684-95.

Kaplan, Morton, A. "The New Great Debate: Traditionalism vs. Science in International Relations," *World Politics* XIX, I (October 1966), I 20.

Kelman, Herbert, C., ed, *International Behaviour*, New York: Holt, Rinchart and Winston, 1965.

Kissinger, Henry A., "Coalition Diplomacy in a Nuclear Age," *Foreign Affairs*, 42, 4(July 1964), 525-45.

Lerner, Daniel., *The Nazi Elite*, Hoover Institute Elite Studies, Stanford: Stanford, University Press, 1951.

McIntosh, Donald S., "Power and Social Control," *The American Political Science Review*, I, VII, 3 (September 1963) 619-31.

McNeil, Elton B., "Psychology and Aggression," *The Journal of Conflict Resolution*, III, 3(September 1959), 195-293.

Mead, Margaret, "National Character," in A.L. Droeber, edl, *Anthropology Today*, Chicago: The University of Chicago Press, 1953.

Miller, D.H., *The Drafting of the Covenant*, Two Vols, New York: Putnam's 1928.

Moore, Barrington, Jr., *Political Power and Social Theory*, Cambridge: Harvard University Press, 1958.

Niebuhr, Reinhold, *Moral Man and Immoral Society*, New York Scribner's, 1948.

Organski, A.F.K. *The Stages of Political Development*, New York: Knopf, 1965.

Powell, Ralph, "China's Bomb Exploitation and Reactions," *Foreign Affairs*, 43, 4(July 1965), 616-25.

Pye, Lucian W., *Politics, Personality and Nation Building: Burma's Search for Identity*, New Haven: Yale University Press, 1962.

Rostow, W.W., *The Stages of Economic Growth*, Cambridge: At the University Press, 1961.

Seabury, Paul, *The Withelmstrase*. Berkeley: University of California Press, 1954.

Singer, J. David, (ed.) *Human Behaviour and International Politics*, Chicago: Rand McNally, 1965.

Tawney, R.H., *Religion and the Rise of Capitalism*, New York: Mentor Books, New American Library, 1953.

Ulam, Adam B., "The Cominform and the People's Democracies, *World Politics III*, 2 (January 1951), 200-17.

Vagts, Alred, "The Balance of Power: Growth of an Idea," *World Politics*, I, (October 1948), 82-101.

Webster, Charles K., *The Foreign Policy of Castlereagh*, 1815 1822, London: Bell, 1947.

Williams, William A., *The Tragedy of American Diplomacy*, Cleveland, World, 1959.

Zagoria, Donald S., *The Sino-Soviet Conflict, 1956-1961*, Princeton: Princeton University Press, 1962.

Index

I

K

L

□□□